100

100

of the world's best

houses

100
of the world's best
houses

images
Publishing

First reprint 2011
The Images Publishing Group Reference Number: 962

Published in Australia in 2002 by
The Images Publishing Group Pty Ltd
ACN 059 734 431
6 Bastow Place, Mulgrave, Victoria 3170, Australia
Telephone (61 3) 9561 5544 Facsimile (61 3) 9561 4860
E-mail: books@images.com.au
Website: www.imagespublishinggroup.com

ISBN: 978 1 86470 435 8

Coordinating Editors: Jodie Davis and Diane Strong
Designed by The Graphic Image Studio Pty Ltd, Mulgrave, Australia
Reprinted by Everbest Printing Co. Ltd. in Hong Kong/China

Contents

Contents continued

Contents continued

Introduction

The private house continues to occupy a unique position both in the history of architecture and human cultural imagination. The house, the domus, the home is at once refuge and shelter. It is the place of communion for the family (and its many contemporary variations), for domestic activities, for living, working, eating and sleeping, and is both a very public and private domain. The distracting delights of cities and social interaction are manifest, but everyone dreams of having a home.

Throughout the Western world, the private house's popularity has remained undiminished during the 20th century. But even so, the current ubiquity of the house in its traditional form—a series of common rooms and separate bedrooms, expressing a domestic culture evolved over centuries—is rife with contradictions. As the American architectural critic Terence Riley has observed, the social conditions and structures that underpinned the development of the private house—privacy, the separation of living and work, the family and the nature of domesticity itself—have all changed drastically. Perhaps more so in the last 50 years than in the preceding four centuries, when the private house began to develop as a popular type. A new and notable generation of house designs—commissioned by forward-thinking clients—is addressing not only critical architectural issues but also the cultural parameters of the private dwelling.

Historically, architects were concerned with providing for the standard nuclear family with parents and children. Now, households are of many types—multigenerational families, co-operative groups, childless couples, single parent families, and so on. The cultural and social definition of the private house is undergoing great change, a transformation that, in itself, can act as a spur to architectural invention. This change is taking place at a time when architecture is also being fuelled by immensely sophisticated new technical and material resources. As well as shifts in social patterns and family structures, the pace of technological development has already established the basis for another profound revolution in domestic life. The increasing availability of computer technology and Internet access has ensured that for many people in the developed world, the home is also the primary place of work. In architectural terms, the reinvention of the home as workspace has implications both for the organisation of space, to mediate between work and domestic activities, and the sphere of mechanical engineering, as houses become 'wired worlds' in response to the increasing demands of electronic data and services.

Another important aspect underpinning the development of houses, particularly since the energy crisis of the 1970s, is the emergence of environmentally responsive design. Many innovative projects have been produced for private houses, as they form a useful starting point for prototypical solutions. In Germany and Scandinavia in particular, green awareness is high and this is reflected in domestic projects that incorporate active and passive environmental control measures, using glass conservatories and photovoltaic panels to generate energy from the sun's light. The results of this vein of ecologically aware investigation ultimately feed into the design of future housing schemes, exemplifying how a one-off project can act as an important test bed for more widely applicable solutions.

Because of its relatively small scale, the house offers fertile scope for formal, spatial and material experimentation. Architecture has witnessed a strong return to the archetype of the private villa, and with the right sort of client; such commissions can offer a level of creative expression that might normally be associated with a larger public building. Imaginative patronage is crucial to this process. All the clients whose houses are described here have shown great enlightenment by giving their architects a free reign to test their vision. The outcome is a memorable and inventive series of buildings.

For clients, the aim is to create a place of shelter and stimulation; for the architect the house is both talisman and testing ground. Despite the ongoing effect of social, cultural and technological changes, the basic house design brief remains constant; yet precisely because it is so thoroughly known, architects can to give full vent to their creativity. The near sacred simplicity of the house also makes it perhaps the only building type for which an architect can exercise complete design control and establish a genuinely intimate client relationship, free from the inhibiting influence of developers, cost managers and bureaucrats.

Different approaches to house design can be discerned in different parts of the world. In the United States and Australia, a house is seen as a powerful statement of success unlike, for instance, in Britain where it is regarded as a first generation ancestral home. In Australia especially, the house has begun to assume a strong sense of regional identity, in response to climate and site and through use of materials. Some of the most intriguing domestic dwellings are being built in Japan, where limitations of space and a willingness to embrace radical concepts expand the boundaries of conventional architectural thinking.

The appeal of the pastoral ideal and its evocation in domestic design still prevails, as affluent city dwellers seek solace in the grandeur of nature. Rather than dominate the natural settings, many houses work in harmony with them, favouring simple, elemental forms—boxes, parallel walls and sheds, albeit refined ones, and extensive zones of transparency. Architecture is used to frame and channel views, allowing terrain to flow around, between or even under built forms. Even in densely developed cities and less glamorous suburban and agricultural zones, the relationship of building to site is a key generator of form.

The houses shown in this volume are designed, in the most part, for well-off clients. But as tends to be the case in architecture, the rich patron, public or private, sets the pace of architectural imagination. The innovations of their architects have lessons for other kinds of home: in clusters, courtyards terraces as well as on individual plots. Imagination is used in many ways: about space, materials and our understanding and appreciation of nature, as well as the changing social dynamic of the family. It is placemaking at its most fundamental. Transformed into a vehicle for personal expression for both client and architect, the house is at once the repository and fulfilment of dreams.

Catherine Slessor
Managing Editor
The Architectural Review

11th & Hill Residence

Santa Monica, California, USA

1

1. A striking deep-blue color and multiple metal rooflines set the stage for a playful and unusual design
2. Kitchen-cabinet pulls were created from discarded cast-iron industrial remnants by Trout who is known for decorative hardware
3. Trout's 'Creature' sculptures are each placed on its own steel pedestal above master bedroom fireplace
4. Living room with angular fireplace leads seamlessly into dining area
5. Bathroom features sinks on a sculptural wood pedestal, and vertical mirrored cabinets that open by pivoting clockwise
6. Second-floor master suite is open and airy, with 'walls' made of coated MDF storage units

Photography: Tom Bonner

2

3

4

5

6

A.J. Diamond, Donald Schmitt and Company

Alumbrera

Mustique, St. Vincent and the Grenadines, West Indies

1

1 Living pavilion verandah
2 Swimming pool and pavilion
3 Living pavilion with louvered doors
4 Living pavilion with diagonal rafters to form coffers
5 Stairs from entrance and bedroom pavilion

Photography: Steven Evans

Ambrosini/Neu Residence

Los Angeles, California, USA

1

1   Façade at rear opening to
    terraced yard
2   Composition of kitchen/master
    bedroom wing
3   Façade along street
4   Detail of corner window condition
    at living room
5   Entry detail

2

3

4

5

6 Interior of two-story living room
7 First floor plan
8 Ground floor plan
9 Dining room/entry area with 'floating' wall divider
10 Kitchen
Photography: courtesy Kanner Architects

6

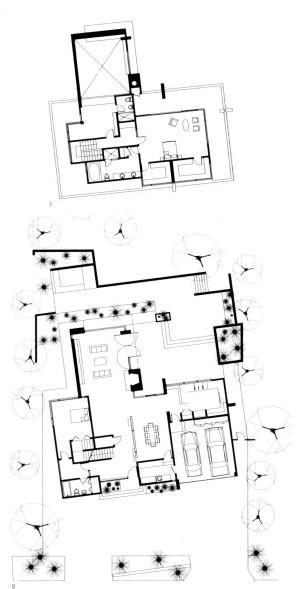

7

8

9

10

Brookes Stacey Randall, Architects

Art House

London, UK

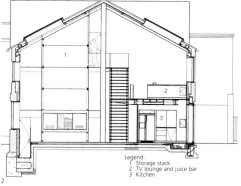

Legend:
1 Storage stack
2 TV lounge and juice bar
3 Kitchen

1   Central space from glazed bridge
2   Section towards storage stack
3   Main space from top of glass stair
4   Central space
5&6   Glazed bridge linking two mezzanine spaces

4

5

6

7 Storage stack serving study, bathrooms, and master bedroom
8 First floor plan
9 Main space from kitchen area
10 Ground floor plan
11 Juice bar
12 Study
13 Master bedroom
14 Master bathroom
Photography: Richard Davies

7

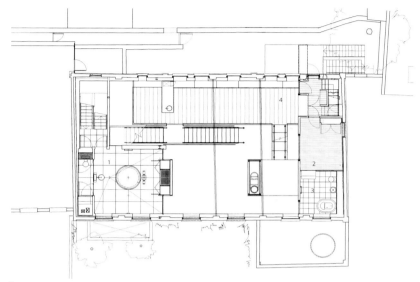
8

9

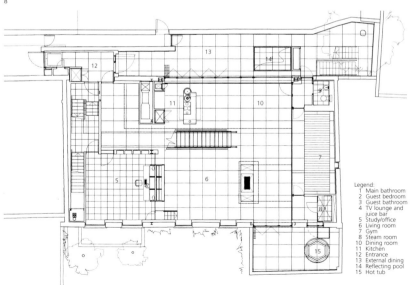
10

Legend:
1 Main bathroom
2 Guest bedroom
3 Guest bathroom
4 TV lounge and juice bar
5 Study/office
6 Living room
7 Gym
8 Steam room
9 Dining room
10 Dining room
11 Kitchen
12 Entrance
13 External dining
14 Reflecting pool
15 Hot tub

11

12

13

14

Art-Nouveau Villa

Sacro Monte, Varese, Italy

1

2

3

4

5

1 The villa is surrounded by a 4,600-square-meter garden
2 West elevation
3 South elevation
4 Triple windows with concrete ornamental pattern characterize the façade
5 Swimming pool in greenhouse

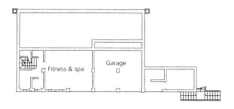

Fitness & spa

Garage

North entrance

Kitchen

Dining room

Living room

Hall

Summer living room

South entry

6

7

8

9

10

6 Ground floor plan
7 Technology and antiques in the winter living room
8 Rhombus pattern flooring contrasts frescoed walls and ceiling, with table designed by Rocco Magnoli
9 Full-height windows lead attention towards landscape outside

10 Japanese geometry and Hoffman style inspire the kitchen furniture
11 Original narrow hall and adjacent verandah have been joined together

Photography: Ezio Prandini

11

Baan Kamonorrathep

Rimtai Saitarn, Mae Rim District, Chiang Mai, Thailand

1

1 Swimming pool in central court
2 Old rice barn
3 Ground floor plan
4 Entrance gate
5 View from south

Legend:
1 Sala
2 Swimming pool
3 Living/dining
4 Pantry
5 Hall
6 Bathroom
7 Outdoor shower
8 Entrance

0   6m

6   Main entrance
7   View from living room
8   Living room
9   Stair leading to upper floor
10 Living room
Photography: Skyline Studio

6

7

8

9

10

Lake/Flato Architects, Inc.

Bartlit Residence

Castle Pines, Colorado, USA

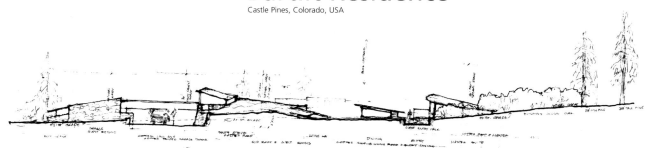

1

2

Legend:
1 Entry
2 Dining room
3 Kitchen
4 Family room
5 Office
6 Bathroom
7 Master closet
8 Master closet
9 Master bedroom
10 Living room
11 Bedroom
12 Bedroom
13 Patio
14 Bedroom
15 Fitness facility
16 Garage
17 Staff quarters
18 Swimming pool

0   60m

1 East elevation
2 Entry walk and house nestled into landscape
3 Thin steel frame of transparent living pavilion
4 Glass living pavilions perched on rocky ridge
5 Glass entry canopy with glimpses of the view
6 Site/floor plan
7 Guest rooms with earthen roofs and open courtyards

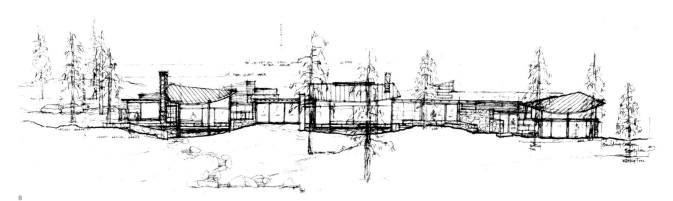

8

9

10

8   West elevation
9   Granite retaining walls penetrate into the interior
10   Cantilevered steel arbor with perforated copper shade screens
11   Pavilion wing roof and operable windows capture breezes
Photography: Hester + Hardaway Photographers

11

Brian Healy Architects and Michael Ryan Architects

Beach House

Long Beach Island, New Jersey, USA

1

1 View of house from beach looking northwest
2 South elevation
3 Building section through main living area and
  master bedroom looking west
4 View of exterior deck off main living area
5 View of house from public walkway to beach
6 Entry court

2

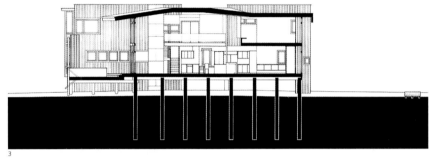

3

4

5

6

7

7 Main living area with master bedroom above
8 Detail view of master bedroom
9 Second level floor plan
10 Kitchen with master bathroom above
11 Main stair and balcony looking west
12 Detail view of kitchen and dining area
Photography: Paul Warchol

8

9

Legend:
1 Stairs
2 Main living area
3 Kitchen
4 Dining area
5 Fireplace
6 Exterior deck
7 Laundry room
8 Bedroom with bath
9 Powder room
10 Elevator

0   10m

10

11

12

Beckhard House

Glen Cove, New York, USA

1

1　South elevation at twilight
2　Design study perspective
3　56-foot glass wall and contrasting white painted siding
4　Floor plan
5　Living room with rough stone fireplace wall
Photography: Nick Wheeler (1,5); Ben Schnall (3)
Drawing: Stanley Abercrombie (2)

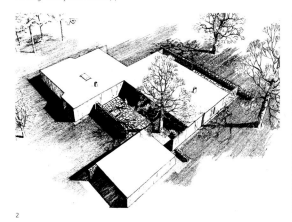

2

Legend:
　1　Courtyard
　2　Living room
　3　Dining room
　4　Kitchen
　5　Master bedroom
　6　Service courtyard
　7　Guest bedroom
　8　Storage
　9　Child's bedroom
10　Child's living room

4

3

5

Rem Koolhaas, Office of Metropolitan Architecture

Bordeaux House

Bordeaux, France

1

44

2

3

4

1 Exterior view
2 Support structures
3 Circular garden
4 Curved walkway

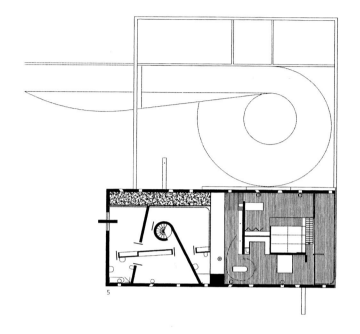

5

6

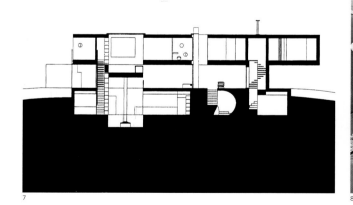

7

8

5	Floor plan	9	Lower office
6	Kitchen	10	Elevator shaft
7	East elevation	11	Office elevator at upper level
8	Bathroom		Photography: Hans Werlemann/Hectic Pictures

9

10

11

Brick Bay House

Warkworth, New Zealand

1

1 Approach to house through Brick Bay farm
2 Context of house with views of Haruaki Gulf
3 Hallway leading to living space from entry foyer
4 Entry foyer with stair to upper living areas and upper bedrooms
5 Copper-clad upper living room sits on carved timber posts above dining area
6 Main living area, with fireplace and tower, opening to views and external living areas

Photography: Mark Klever

Brody House

Florida, USA

1

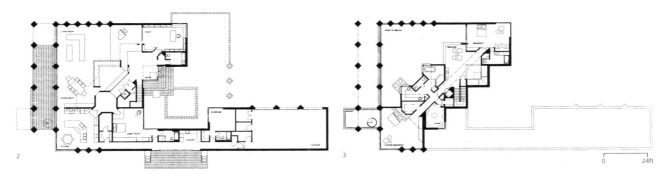

2

3

0   24ft

1   Bayside elevation
2   First floor plan
3   Second floor plan
4   Entry

4

5   Dining room with master bedroom above
6   Living room
7   Master bedroom
8   Bay view from study
9   Dining room light fixture
10 Second floor reading room

Photography: Ed Zealy

5

6

7

8

9

10

Burd Haward Marston Architects
Brooke Coombes House
London, UK

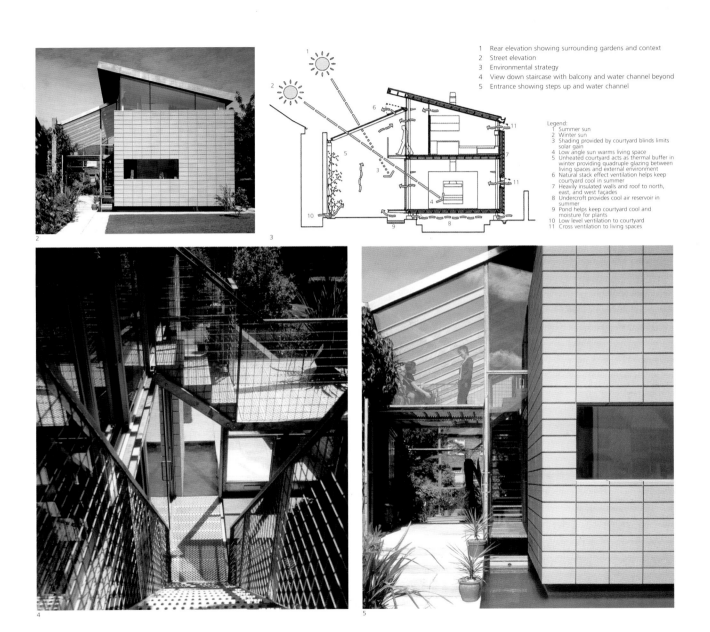

1 Rear elevation showing surrounding gardens and context
2 Street elevation
3 Environmental strategy
4 View down staircase with balcony and water channel beyond
5 Entrance showing steps up and water channel

Legend:
1 Summer sun
2 Winter sun
3 Shading provided by courtyard blinds limits solar gain
4 Low angle sun warms living space
5 Unheated courtyard acts as thermal buffer in winter providing quadruple glazing between living spaces and external environment
6 Natural stack effect ventilation helps keep courtyard cool in summer
7 Heavily insulated walls and roof to north, east, and west façades
8 Undercroft provides cool air reservoir in summer
9 Pond helps keep courtyard cool and moisture for plants
10 Low level ventilation to courtyard
11 Cross ventilation to living spaces

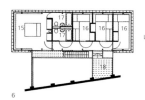

6

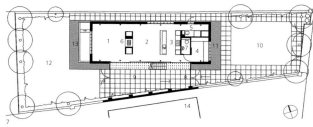

7

Legend:
1 Living room
2 Dining room
3 Kitchen
4 Study
5 Utility
6 Fireplace
7 WC
8 Entrance
9 Courtyard
10 Front garden
11 Upper pond
12 Rear garden
13 Lower pond
14 Adjacent property
15 Master bedroom
16 Children's bedroom
17 Bathroom
18 Balcony

6 First floor plan
7 Ground floor plan
8 View along first floor corridor with sliding doors to courtyard on left
9 View from living area into courtyard
10 View from courtyard into living area
Photography: Charlotte Wood

8

9

10

Adrian Maserow Architects

Brouwer House

Gauteng, South Africa

1

2

3

4

1 Line sketch of street elevation
2 Entrance façade
3 Outdoor 'Kgotla'
4 Front door
5 Courtyard and raised pool
6 Internal stairway
7 Ground floor plan
8 Entrance breezeway
Photography: courtesy Adrian
Maserow Architects

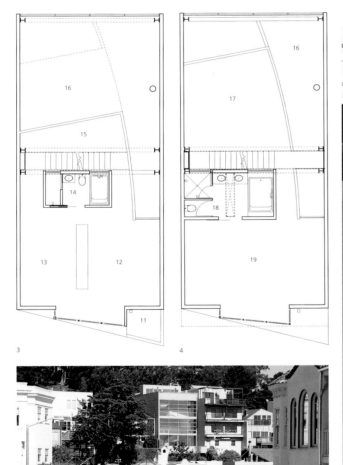

7   View into living area from deck
8   Living area
9   Master bedroom
10   Guest bath
11   Kitchen and dining
Photography: Claudio Santini, Alan Geller

7

8

9

10

11

Burns Residence

Venice, California, USA

1

2

3

4

5

6

1 Canal side exterior view
2 Garden
3 Deck
4 Library
5 Living room with kitchen beyond
6 Stair detail
Photo credit: courtesy Glen Irani Architects

Ahrends Burton and Koralek

Burton House

Kentish Town, London, UK

1

2

3

4

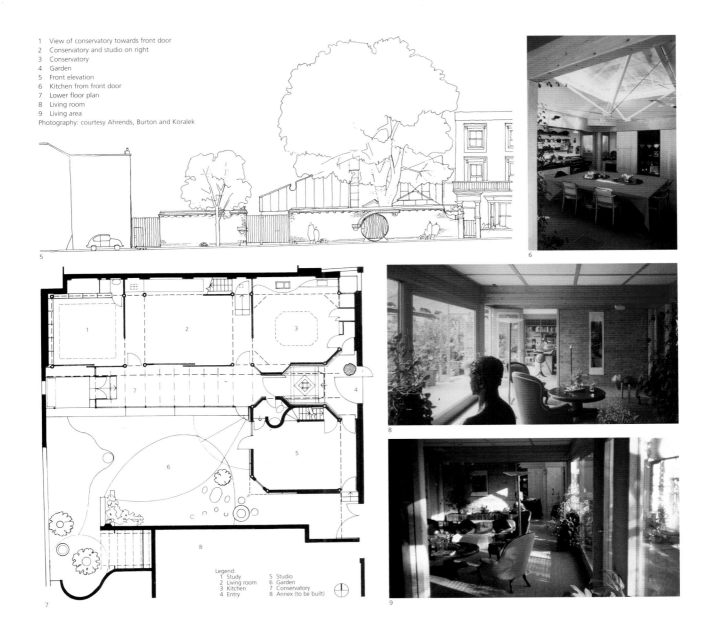

1   View of conservatory towards front door
2   Conservatory and studio on right
3   Conservatory
4   Garden
5   Front elevation
6   Kitchen from front door
7   Lower floor plan
8   Living room
9   Living area
Photography: courtesy Ahrends, Burton and Koralek

5

7

Legend:
1 Study   5 Studio
2 Living room   6 Garden
3 Kitchen   7 Conservatory
4 Entry   8 Annex (to be built)

6

8

9

Caner/Beier Residence

Napa County, California, USA

1

2

3

1 Uphill view from northwest
2 Overview from southwest
3 Terrace from southeast
4 Dining trellis and tower

4

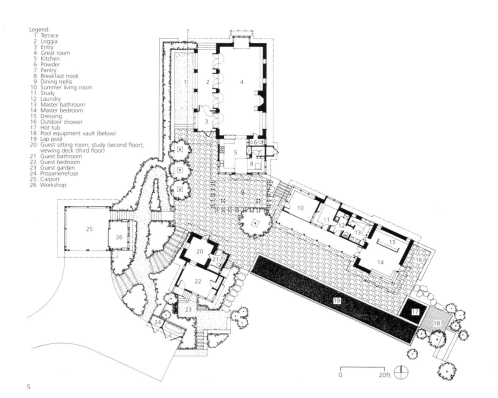

Legend:
1 Terrace
2 Loggia
3 Entry
4 Great room
5 Kitchen
6 Powder
7 Pantry
8 Breakfast nook
9 Dining trellis
10 Summer living room
11 Study
12 Laundry
13 Master bathroom
14 Master bedroom
15 Dressing
16 Outdoor shower
17 Hot tub
18 Pool equipment vault (below)
19 Lap pool
20 Guest sitting room; study (second floor);
   viewing deck (third floor)
21 Guest bathroom
22 Guest bedroom
23 Guest garden
24 Propane/refuse
25 Carport
26 Workshop

5

0   20ft

6

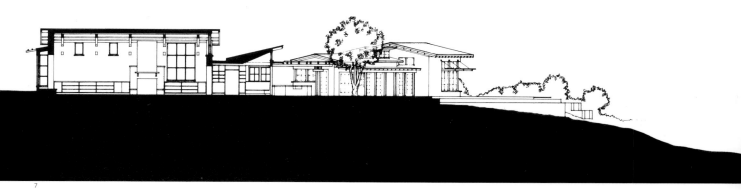

7

72

8

9

10

11

12

5   Floor plan
6   Dutch door at entry
7   North–south section
8   Kitchen and breakfast nook
9   Guest bathroom
10 Master bathroom
11 Kitchen
12 Master bedroom
Photography: Ed Caldwell

Canyon Residence

Los Angeles, California, USA

1

1 Full view of rear façade from backyard and pool
2 Double-story living room from backyard
3 Bedroom wing
4 Front façade from street
5 Second floor plan
6 First floor plan
7 Lower level floor plan

2

3

4

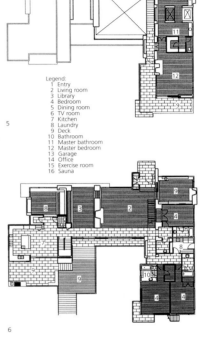

Legend:
1 Entry
2 Living room
3 Library
4 Bedroom
5 Dining room
6 TV room
7 Kitchen
8 Laundry
9 Deck
10 Bathroom
11 Master bathroom
12 Master bedroom
13 Garage
14 Office
15 Exercise room
16 Sauna

5

6

7

0   16ft

8

10

11

8   View from master bedroom down
    to middle-level terrace
9   West elevation
10 'Floating' stair to master bedroom
11 Kitchen

12 North elevation
13 East elevation
14 South elevation
15 Living room
Photo credit: Tim Street-Porter

12

13

14

15

Cape Schanck House

Cape Schanck, Victoria, Australia

1

2

3

1 View from courtyard
2 Level two floor plan
3 Level one floor plan
4 View from east
5 Living room towards courtyard
6 View from south
7 Living room towards kitchen
Photography: Tim Griffith

4

5

6

7

Cesar Pelli & Associates Inc

Carmel House

Pebble Beach, California, USA

1

2

3

4

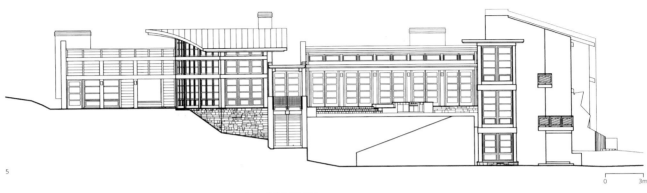

5

0   3m

6

7

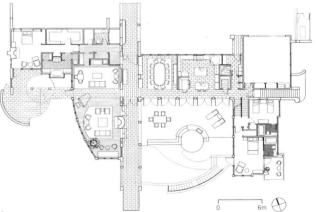

9

0   6m

8

1   Front entrance
2   View from south
3   Detail of guest wing elevation
4   Daytime view of courtyard
5   South elevation
6   Kitchen with Aga stove and pizza oven
7   View from logia to Point Lobos
8   Living room
9   Site plan
Photography: Timothy Hursley (1,2,4,6–8); Cesar Pelli (3)

Sean Godsell

Carter/Tucker House

Breamlea, Victoria, Australia

1

2

3

4

5

6

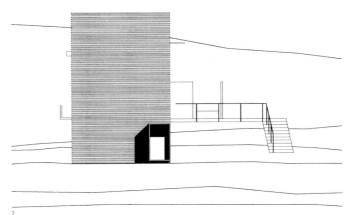

7

8

9

10

Carwill House

Stratton, Vermont, USA

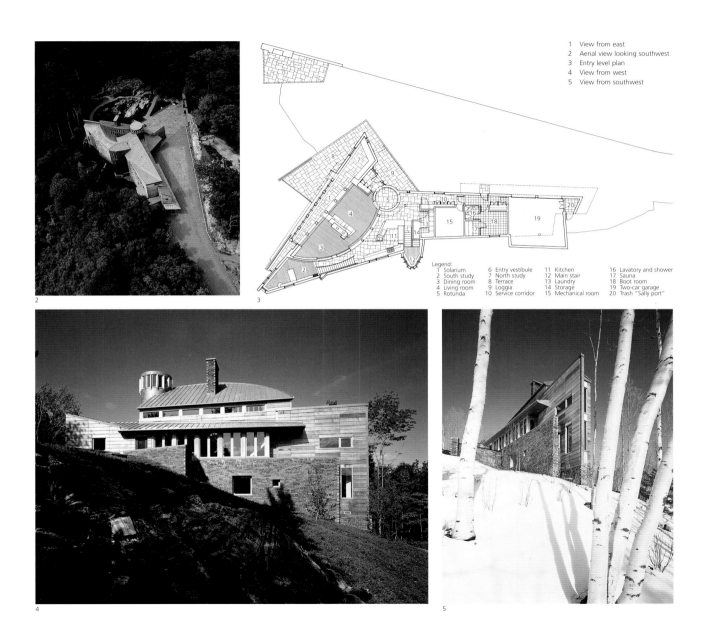

1 View from east
2 Aerial view looking southwest
3 Entry level plan
4 View from west
5 View from southwest

Legend:
1 Solarium
2 South study
3 Dining room
4 Living room
5 Rotunda
6 Entry vestibule
7 North study
8 Terrace
9 Loggia
10 Service corridor
11 Kitchen
12 Main stair
13 Laundry
14 Storage
15 Mechanical room
16 Lavatory and shower
17 Sauna
18 Boot room
19 Two-car garage
20 Trash "Sally port"

6　Longitudinal section through living/dining room
7　Main stair window
8　Cross section through dining room
9　Tall interior spaces spin off from a cylindrical node
10　Fireplace with appended china cabinet, separates dining/living areas
Photography: Wayne N.T. Fujii

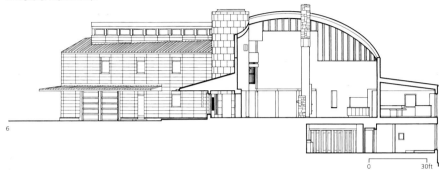

6

0　　　　30ft

7

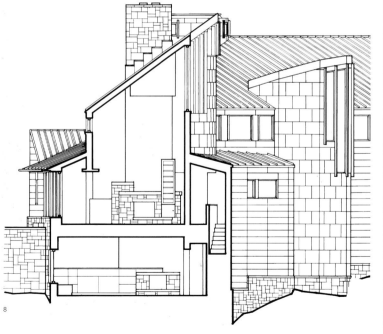

8

9

10

Architecture Research Office

Colorado House

Telluride, Colorado, USA

1

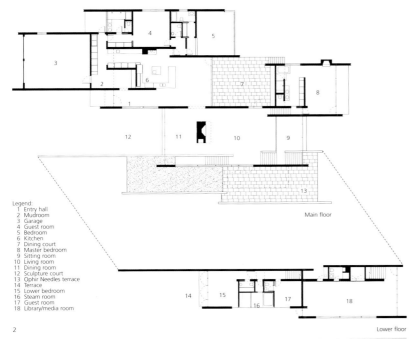

Main floor

Legend:
1 Entry hall
2 Mudroom
3 Garage
4 Guest room
5 Bedroom
6 Kitchen
7 Dining court
8 Master bedroom
9 Sitting room
10 Living room
11 Dining room
12 Sculpture court
13 Ophir Needles terrace
14 Terrace
15 Lower bedroom
16 Steam room
17 Guest room
18 Library/media room

Lower floor

1 Exterior view
2 Floor plan
3 Entry
4 Wall ends

2

3

4

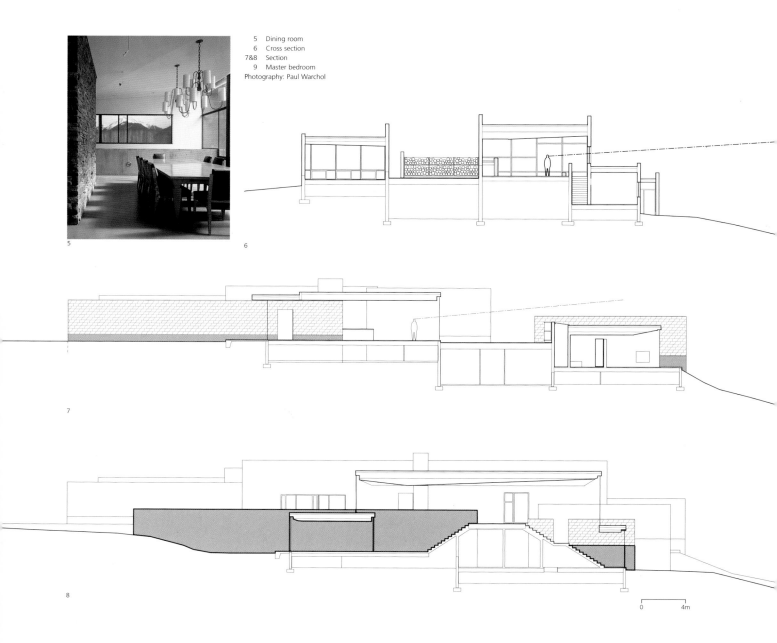

5 Dining room
6 Cross section
7&8 Section
9 Master bedroom
Photography: Paul Warchol

5

6

7

8

0   4m

9

McInturff Architects
Cozzens Residence
Washington DC, USA

1

1 Potomac River elevation at night
2 Teak sunscreens on river elevation
3 Section
4 View room

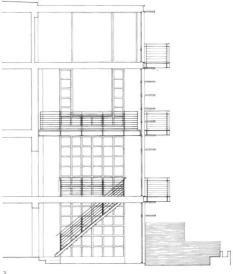

5

5 Double-height view room and bridge from study
6 Bridge from study
7 Dining room with kitchen beyond
8 Master bedroom
9 Second floor plan
10 First floor plan
Photography: Julia Heine

6

7

8

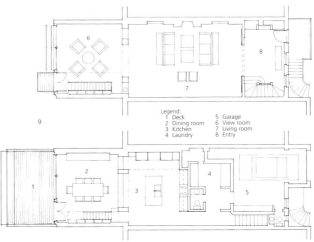

9

10

Legend:
1 Deck
2 Dining room
3 Kitchen
4 Laundry
5 Garage
6 View room
7 Living room
8 Entry

Dr Ken Shuttleworth, Architect

Crescent House

Wiltshire, UK

1

1 Exterior view
2 Site plan
3 Exterior view

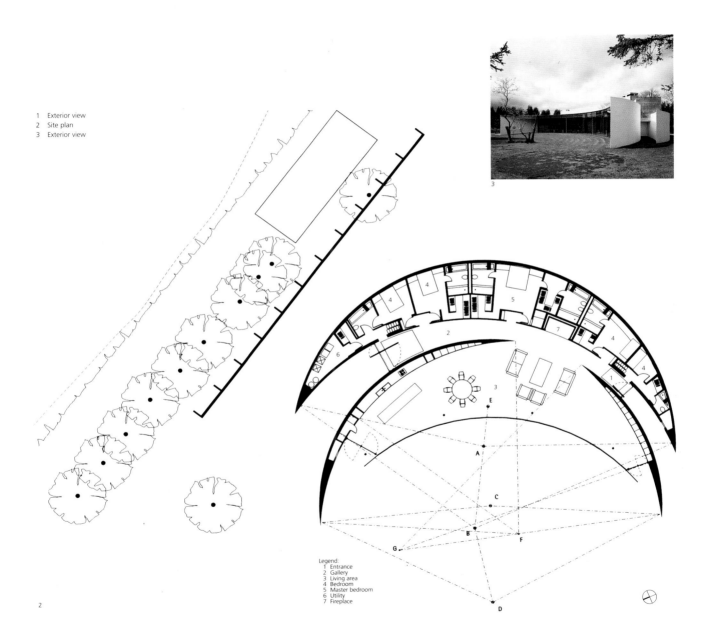

3

2

Legend:
1 Entrance
2 Gallery
3 Living area
4 Bedroom
5 Master bedroom
6 Utility
7 Fireplace

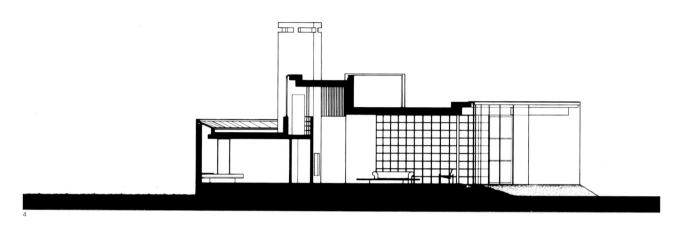

4

5

6

10

OJMR Architects

Defeo House Renovation

Venice, California, USA

1 Slight angles, sloping roof lines, and tilted planes in design allow natural light to modulate throughout different rooms

2 Glass panel walls establish a connection between the house and its natural surrounding, merging both private and public spaces

3 Master bedroom leads into bathroom seamlessly without any division

4 First floor plan after renovation and expansion process

5 Height expansion of ceiling and walls offers a spacious and open feeling to the living room

6 Large glass windows act as walls to allow natural light to enter living room

7 Kitchen maximizes use of cooking area with more countertop space and cabinetry

Photography: Maria Antonia Viteri

3

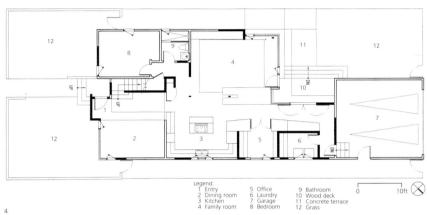

4

Legend:
1 Entry	5 Office	9 Bathroom	
2 Dining room	6 Laundry	10 Wood deck	
3 Kitchen	7 Garage	11 Concrete terrace	
4 Family room	8 Bedroom	12 Grass	

0   10ft

5

6

7

Dr Manke Residence

Melbeck, Germany

1

1 View from landscaped garden with pond
2 Side view of terrace wall
3 Ground floor plan
4 Side view with entrance to service rooms
5 Front façade with entrance

2

3

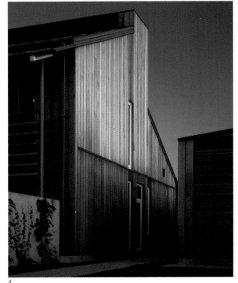

4

5

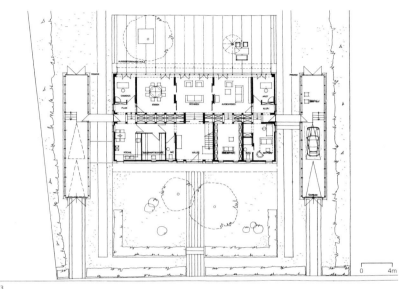

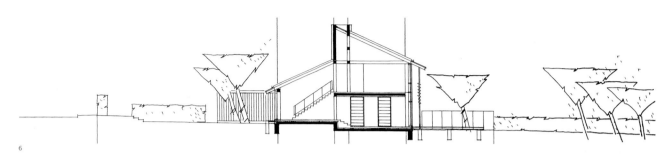

6

7

Photography: Dominik Reipka

8

9

10

Drake House

Westchester, New York, USA

1

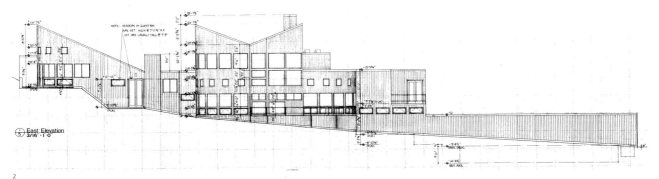

East Elevation
3/16" · 1'·0

2

3

4

5

6

7

1 Approach to house
2 Long elevation
3 Side
4 Entrance
5 Dining room
6 Living room
7 Pool
Photography: Paul Warchol

William Morgan Architects PA
Drysdale Residence
Atlantic Beach, Florida, USA

1

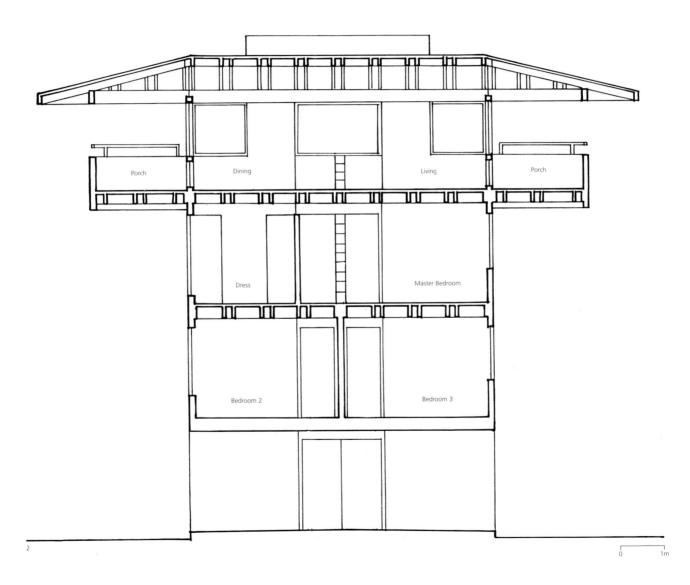

1   Exterior view from north
2   East–west section

Porch

Dining

Living

Porch

Dress

Master Bedroom

Bedroom 2

Bedroom 3

2

0   1m

3 Fourth floor plan
4 Third floor plan
5 Interior view of kitchen
6 Interior stairs
7 Exterior view from east
8 Interior view of fourth floor
Photography: George Cott

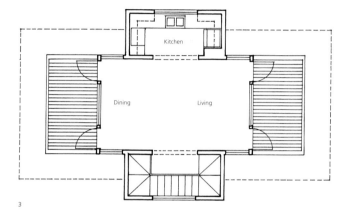

Kitchen

Dining

Living

3

5

6

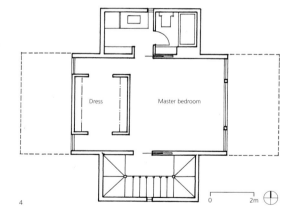

Dress

Master bedroom

4

0   2m

7

Gallery for Contemporary Art

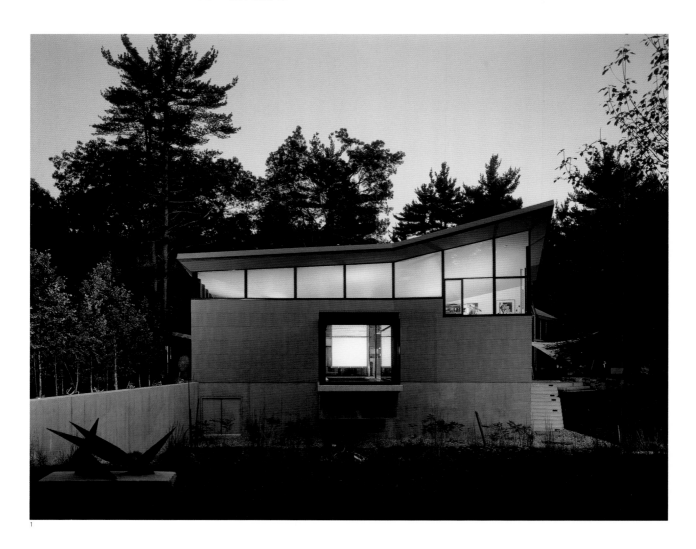

1

1 View of gallery from terraced sculpture garden
2 View of zinc-clad main entry to gallery
3 Detail of east court
4 Second floor plan
5 View of west court showing transition from cedar-lined siding to zinc-clad shingles and terraced sculpture garden beyond
6 Ground floor plan

2

3

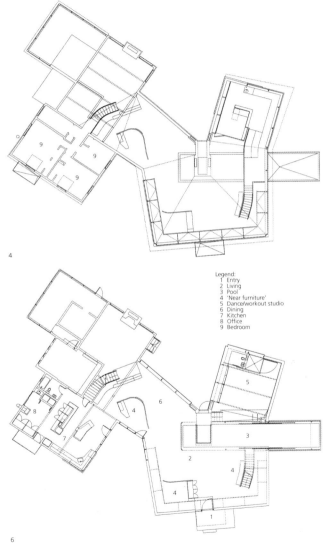

4

Legend:
1 Entry
2 Living
3 Pool
4 'Near furniture'
5 Dance/workout studio
6 Dining
7 Kitchen
8 Office
9 Bedroom

5

6

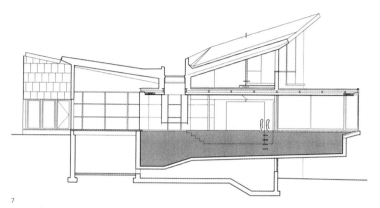

7

8

9

10

11

7 Cross section shows pool inserted partially within space of gallery and cantilevered over sculpture garden (right)

8 Interior view of cantilevered portion of pool taken from second floor office

9 Kitchen bar and cabinetry beyond

10 View from end of glass-mosaic tiled pool looking towards the suspended impluvium

11 Interior view of gallery, pool, and bridge to high-tech office

12 View of dance studio looking towards west court through patterned thermal glass

Photography: Bruce T. Martin

12

Olson Sundberg Kundig Allen Architects

Garden House

Atherton, California, USA

1   South façade
2   South façade from lower yard
3   South façade with water feature
4   Site plan
5   Detail of area between living room pavilion
    (temple) and gallery

2

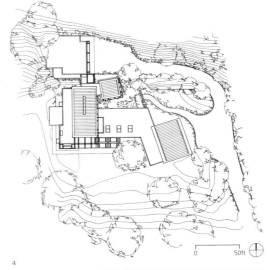

4

3

5

6   Detail view of living room with entry at left
7   View from entry down gallery
8   Main floor plan
9   General view of living room (temple)
10 Gallery adjoining living room (temple)
Photography: Bruce van Inwegen (1,2,7,9); Paul Warchol (3,5,6,10)

6

7

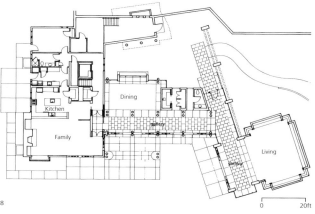

8

9

10

Parsonson Architects
Gibbs House
Eastbourne, Wellington, New Zealand

1

1 View of living section of house from forest
2 View across living room deck
3 Site plan
4 View from road
5 View of house from forest

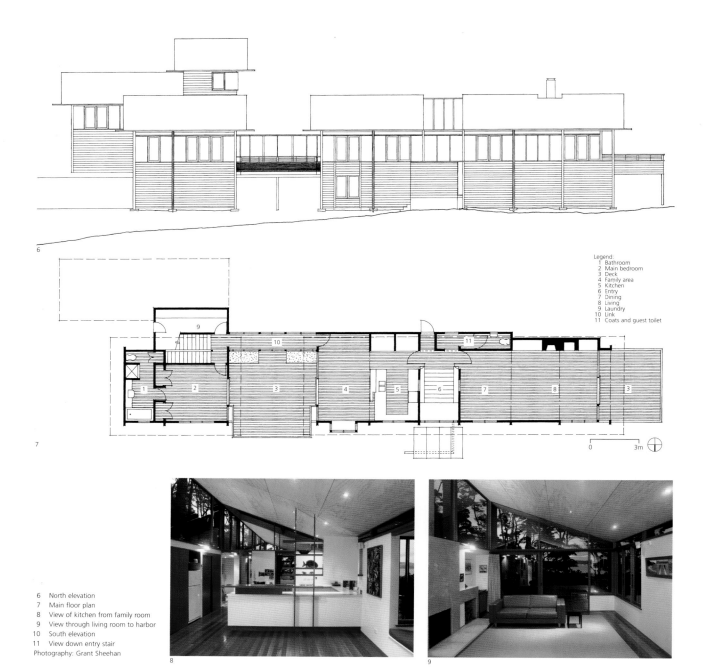

Legend:
1 Bathroom
2 Main bedroom
3 Deck
4 Family area
5 Kitchen
6 Entry
7 Dining
8 Living
9 Laundry
10 Link
11 Coats and guest toilet

0   3m

6   North elevation
7   Main floor plan
8   View of kitchen from family room
9   View through living room to harbor
10   South elevation
11   View down entry stair
Photography: Grant Sheehan

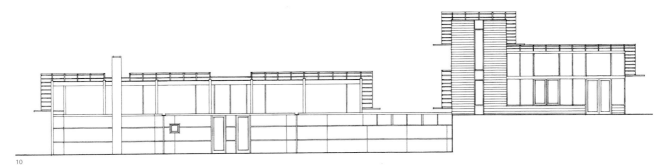

10

11

Green Street Residence

Melbourne, Victoria, Australia

1

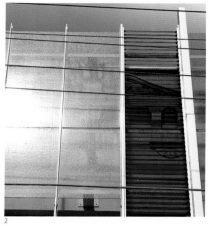

2

3

1 Front street elevation
2 Detail of street elevation
3 Looking down to studio from stair
4 Section
5 Kitchen and dining area
6 Living area

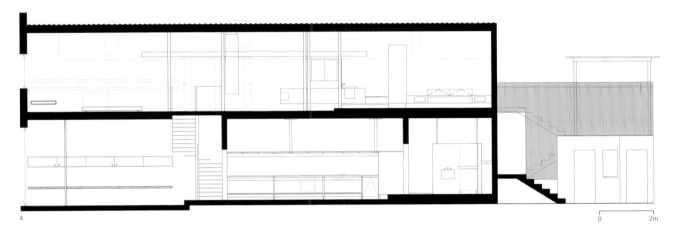

4

0   2m

5

6

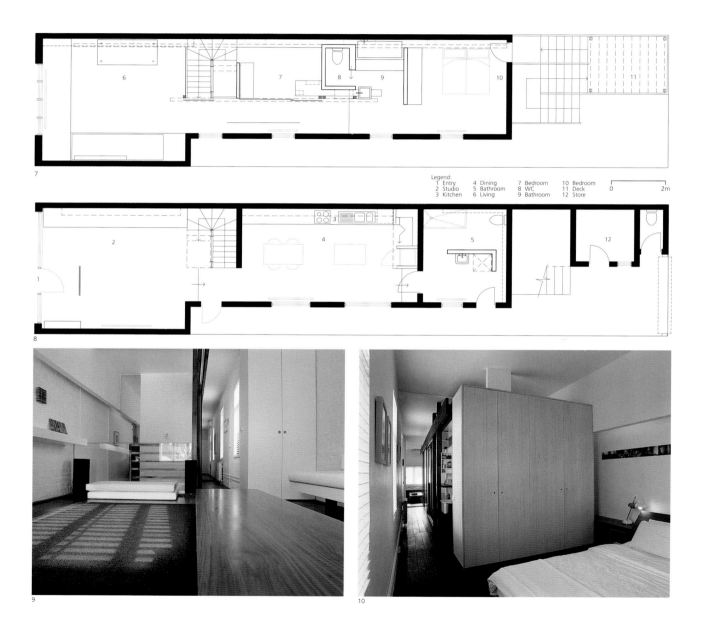

Legend:
1 Entry 4 Dining 7 Bedroom 10 Bedroom
2 Studio 5 Bathroom 8 WC 11 Deck
3 Kitchen 6 Living 9 Bathroom 12 Store

0   2m

11

Greenwood House

Galiano Island, British Columbia, Canada

1	West wall
2&3	West elevation
4	Gallery towards entrance
5	Floor plan and southwest elevation
6	Living room
7	Master bedroom
8	Gallery looking towards kitchen

Photography: John Fulker

4

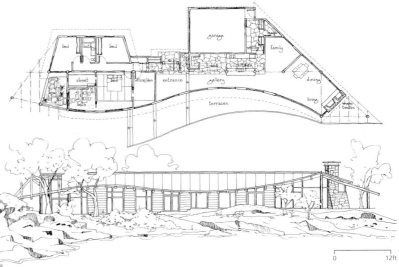

5

6

7

8

Harry Seidler & Associates
Hamilton House
Vaucluse, New South Wales, Australia

1

1   Entrance drive and view of side terraces
2   Entrance drive
3   Entry to forespace and circular stair
4   View of side terraces
5   Terraces on view side
6   Curved entrance drive

7	Dining room	12	Kitchen (granite and stainless steel)
8	Living space	13	First floor plan
9	Space over circular stair	14	Circular entry stair
10	View of Sydney from bedroom	15	Main bathroom
11	Ground floor plan		

Photo credit: courtesy Harry Seidler & Associates

7

8

9

10

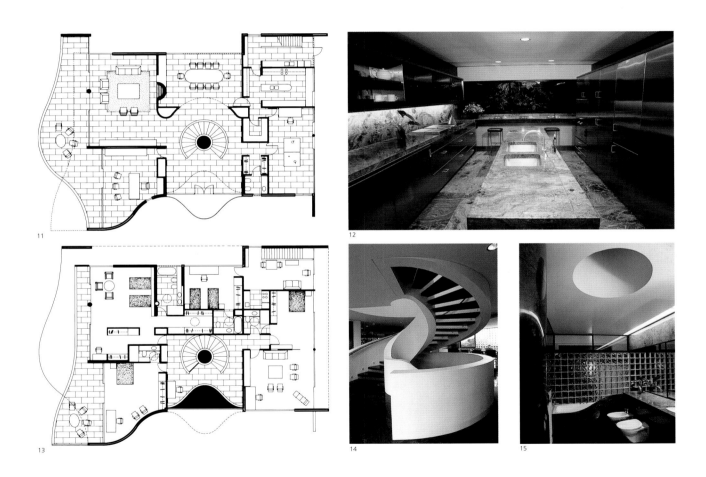

11

12

13

14

15

Hammond Residence

Sunshine Coast, Queensland, Australia

1

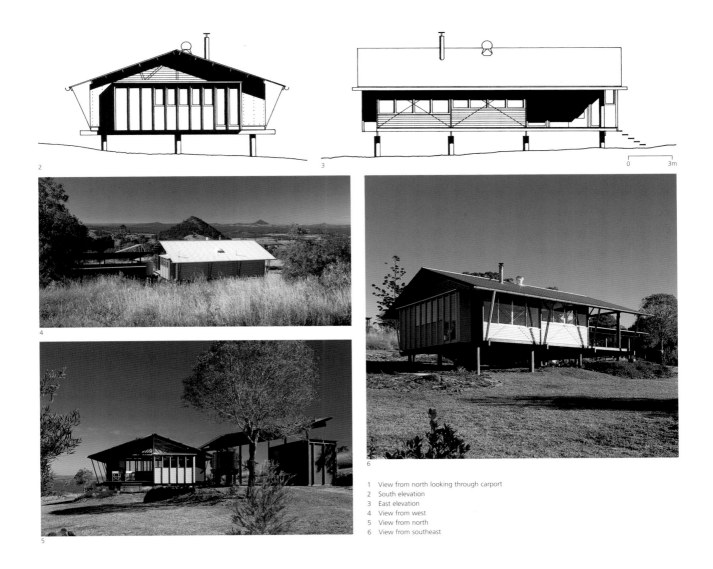

2

3

0   3m

4

6

5

1   View from north looking through carport
2   South elevation
3   East elevation
4   View from west
5   View from north
6   View from southeast

7　　Interior looking north
8　　Floor plan
9　　Interior looking south
10　 Looking east from bedroom to study desk
11　 Kitchen viewed from entry deck
Photography: John Gollings (1); Adrian Boddy (4–6);
Reiner Blunck (7,9–11)

7

8

9

10

11

Looney Ricks Kiss

Harbor Town Residence

Memphis, Tennessee, USA

1

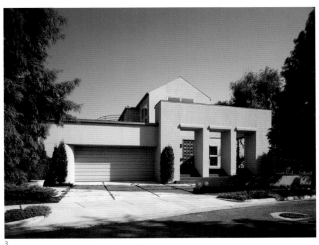

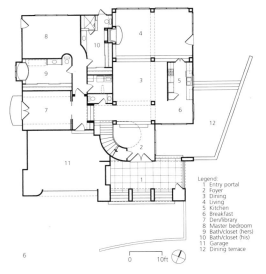

2

3

4

5

1　Side view overlooking dining terrace
2　Pool-terrace area with pergola
3　Entry portal and recessed garage
4　Raised foyer
5　Stepped-down living area
6　First floor plan

Photography: Jeffrey Jacobs/Architectural Photography, Inc.

6

Legend:
1　Entry portal
2　Foyer
3　Dining
4　Living
5　Kitchen
6　Breakfast
7　Den/library
8　Master bedroom
9　Bath/closet (hers)
10　Bath/closet (his)
11　Garage
12　Dining terrace

0　　10ft

House 2 for Two Architects

San Miguel de Allende, Mexico

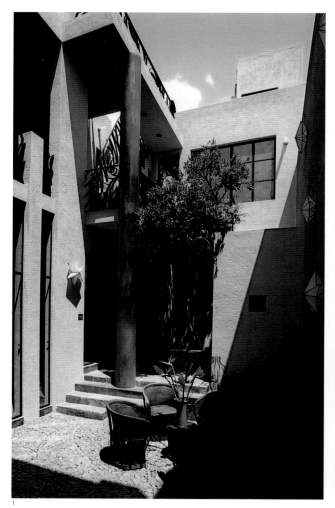

1   Courtyard view from entry   5   Living and dining rooms
2   Courtyard view towards entry   6   First floor plan
3   Living room   7   Second floor plan
4   Master bedroom   Photography: Steven House

3

4

6

5

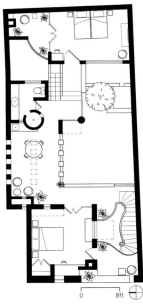

7

0   8ft

House at Toro Canyon

Montecito, California, USA

1

2

3

4

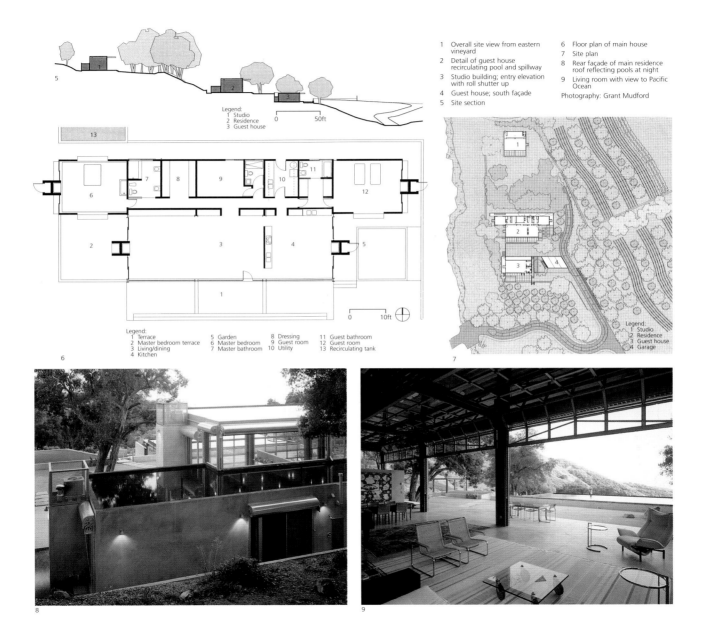

Legend:
1 Studio
2 Residence
3 Guest house

0   50ft

13

6

2

3

1

7   8

9   10   11   12

5

0   10ft

Legend:
1 Terrace   5 Garden   8 Dressing   11 Guest bathroom
2 Master bedroom terrace   6 Master bedroom   9 Guest room   12 Guest room
3 Living/dining   7 Master bathroom   10 Utility   13 Recirculating tank
4 Kitchen

6

1 Overall site view from eastern vineyard
2 Detail of guest house recirculating pool and spillway
3 Studio building; entry elevation with roll shutter up
4 Guest house; south façade
5 Site section

6 Floor plan of main house
7 Site plan
8 Rear façade of main residence roof reflecting pools at night
9 Living room with view to Pacific Ocean

Photography: Grant Mudford

Legend:
1 Studio
2 Residence
3 Guest house
4 Garage

7

8

9

House for Sonoran Desert

Scottsdale, Arizona, USA

1

1 Overall view from entrance side
2 Night view from golf course
3 Ornamental bronze garage doors
4 Three-dimensional copper fascia
5 Lower garage driveway continues to upper garages beyond, note curvilinear stone entry
6 Bronze sculpture with silver leaf and black granite
7 Detail of entry sculpture

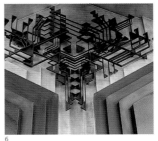

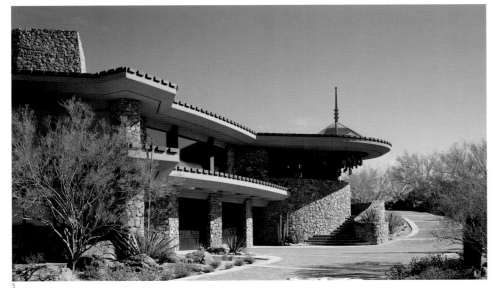

8

9

10

8   Curved gallery featuring custom niches and glass sculptures
9   Custom lamps and dining chandelier designed by architect
10 Ceiling light cove carries out circular character
11 Custom dining table curved at house radius
12 Main level floor plan
13 Lower level floor plan
Photography: Dino Tonn

Legend:
 1 Master bathroom
 2 Dressing room
 3 Spa
 4 Pool
 5 Master suite
 6 Exercise room
 7 Office/library
 8 Garage
 9 Informal dining
10 Kitchen
11 Utility room
12 Dining/buffet
13 Media room
14 Bar
15 Entry
16 Living room
17 Bedroom
18 Guest suite

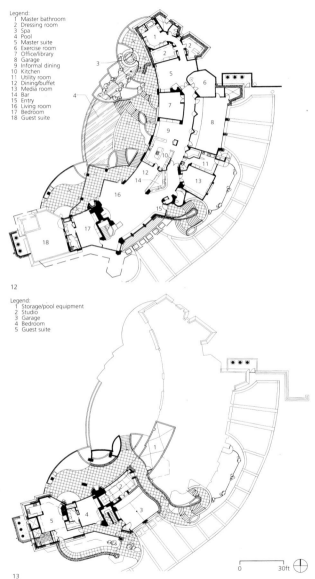

12

Legend:
 1 Storage/pool equipment
 2 Studio
 3 Garage
 4 Bedroom
 5 Guest suite

11

13

0   30ft

House for the Future

Museum of Welsh Life, St Fagans, Cardiff, Wales, UK

1

1 View from garden to south
2 North façade
3 Section
4 Aerial view
5 Ground floor plan

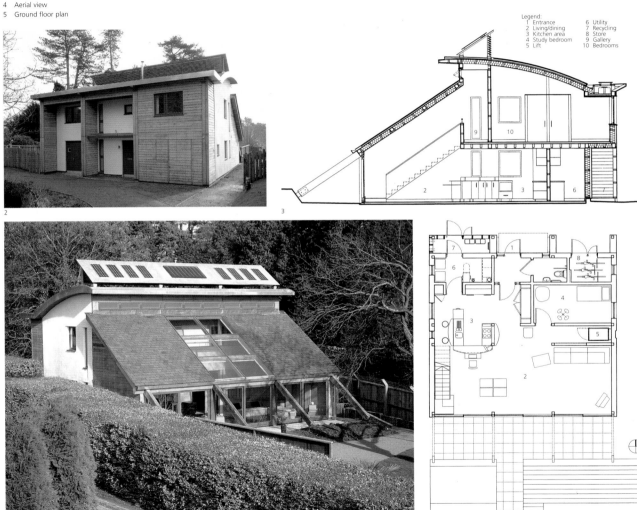

Legend:
1 Entrance   6 Utility
2 Living/dining   7 Recycling
3 Kitchen area   8 Store
4 Study bedroom   9 Gallery
5 Lift   10 Bedrooms

2

3

4

5

6   Living area
7   Gallery
8   South elevation
9   Open-plan kitchen area
10 Living area
Photography: courtesy National Museums and Galleries of Wales

7

8

9

10

House in Aggstall

Bavaria, Germany

1

2

3

1 View from east
2 View from north
3 View from southwest
4 View from south
5 Living room

6 Detail of base
7 Bedroom
8 Stairs
Photography: Michael Heinrich

4

5

6

7

8

Satoshi Okada architects

House in Mt Fuji

Fujiyama, Yamanashi Prefecture, Japan

1

1 Building as a shadow
2 Roof line along terrain from street
3 Site plan
4 Diagonal wall from entrance porch into living room
5 Façade in high summer

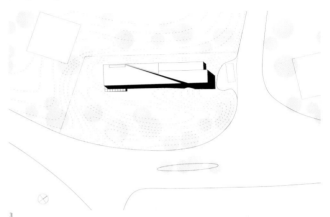

6

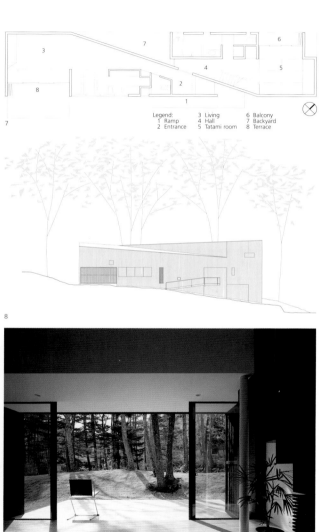

Legend:
1 Ramp   3 Living   6 Balcony
2 Entrance   4 Hall   7 Backyard
5 Tatami room 8 Terrace

7

8

9

6   Living room towards entrance
7   First floor plan
8   Southeast elevation
9   Living room towards terrace
10   Kitchen towards dining area
Photography: Katsuhisa Kida (9,10);
Hiroyuki Hirai (1,2,5,6); Satoshi Okada (4)

10

Mark Simon, FAIA & James C. Childress, FAIA, Centerbrook Architects and Planners

House in the Connecticut Hills

Connecticut, USA

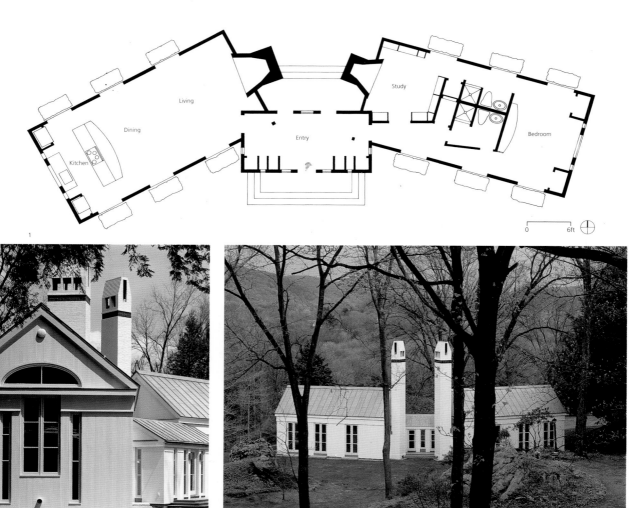

1

2

3

4

5

6

7

8

1   Floor plan
2   Exterior detailing is inspired by Greek revival architecture
3   House nestles into hillside site
4   Entry hall allows access to private and public realms of house
5   Kitchen activity is hidden behind raised island cabinetry
6   Corridor from entry with view towards bedroom
7   Master bedroom
8   Living room forms and furniture reflect simple detailing
Photography: Timothy Hursley

Jefferson B. Riley, FAIA & Charles G. Mueller, AIA, Centerbrook Architects and Planners

House in the Hudson Valley

New York, USA

1   Covered arcade to additions provides an intimate entry through herb garden as well as protection from browsing deer

2&3 Addition of garage, great room, and gym, which appear as connected barns when viewed from the road, command hilltop panorama of pond and mountain

4   Forested great room merges with outdoors; latticed roof overhang shades tall corner windows during summer days

5   Second floor bunkroom is poised like a tree house

6   First floor plan

7   Great room recalls mountain lodges and mysterious forests, providing a welcome retreat from city life

8   Kitchen in existing farmhouse was remodeled with Shaker-style cabinets and granite countertops bearing local fruit shapes

9   Steam bath and Jacuzzi tub continue natural forms of this getaway

Photography: Brian Vanden Brink

5

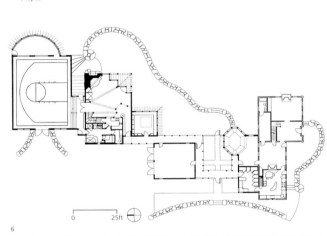

0   25ft

6

7

8

9

Alexander Gorlin Architect

House in the Rocky Mountains

Genesee, Colorado, USA

1

1 General view of house on a rocky outcrop
2 Entrance façade with white curved wall
3 Site plan
4 Building protects roofed terrace
5 House exposes open dynamic elevations towards sea to west
6 Skewed steel columns are cable-stayed and footed directly to granite; they accentuate the project's language of tension and suspension

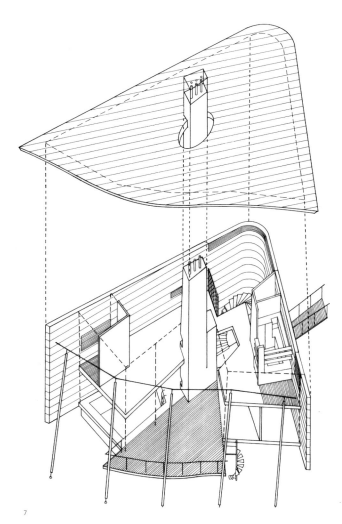

7

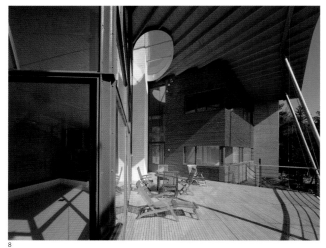

8

9

10

Kim Young-Sub + Kunchook-Moonhwa Architects

J Residence

Seodaeshin-dong, Pusan, Korea

1

2

3

1 Front view
2 View from street
3 Overall view of house
4 Second floor plan
5 Entrance
6 Access to porch
7 Staircase seen from above
8 General view of living room
Photography: Kim Jae-Kyung

Legend:
1 Bedroom
2 Lawn
3 Small music room

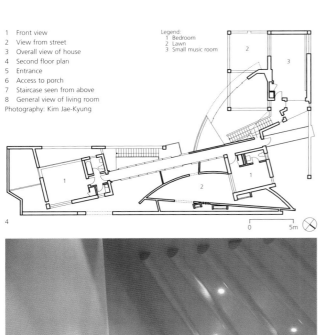

0   5m

Daryl Jackson Architects

Jackson House

New South Wales, Australia

1 Cut edges, deep reveals
2 Beach and bush
3 Courtyard stair and tank
4 Living in the sun
5 Heat and light—living with the elements
6 Overlay; the house as the diagram
7 Long room and wall
Photography: Reiner Blunck

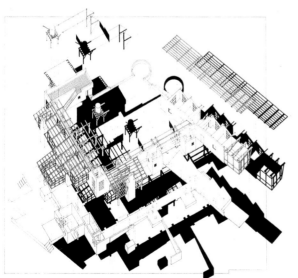

4

5

6

7

Escher GuneWardena Architecture, Inc.

Jamie Residence

Pasadena, USA

1

2

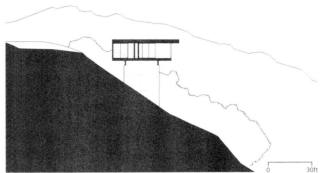

3

4

5

6

1 The 2000 sq ft residence lofted above the steep hillside on two concrete piers, seen from the street below
2 Balcony, accessible from living, dining and kitchen areas, with dramatic panorama
3 Section
4 The house as a floating lantern over the city at night
5 The house, resting on two piers, is connected to the road by a bridge
6 Driveway bridge leads to garage, located at the center of the house

7 Floorplan (storage and utility spaces are located in enclosed volumes)
8 Living room at east end of the house with views of the San Gabriel Mountains
9 Dining area at the crossing of the public and private areas of the house
10 Family room at west end of the house with views of the San Rafael Hills
11 View through the entire house—volumes on the right contain storage spaces and garage.

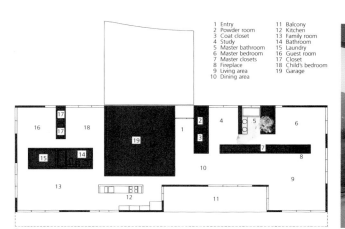

1 Entry
2 Powder room
3 Coat closet
4 Study
5 Master bathroom
6 Master bedroom
7 Master closets
8 Fireplace
9 Living area
10 Dining area
11 Balcony
12 Kitchen
13 Family room
14 Bathroom
15 Laundry
16 Guest room
17 Closet
18 Child's bedroom
19 Garage

7

8

9

10

11

John Daish Architects + The Walls Organisation (T.W.O.)

Kebbell House

Te Horo, Kapiti Coast, New Zealand

1

2

1 Northeast elevation
2 Northwest elevation
3 Lap pool
4 Bathroom
5 Front entry
6 Mezzanine floor and void over library
Photography: Paul McCredie (3–5);
Daniel Watt (1,2,6)

Lorcan O'Herlihy Architects

Kline Residence

Malibu, California, USA

1

2

3

1 View of house from street
2 Studio
3 Exterior view of entry
4 Master bedroom

4

5

6

7

8

5   View to Pacific Ocean from master bedroom
6   Dining Room with kitchen beyond
7   Entry
8   Master bathroom

9   Second floor plan
10 First floor plan
Photography: Tom Bonner

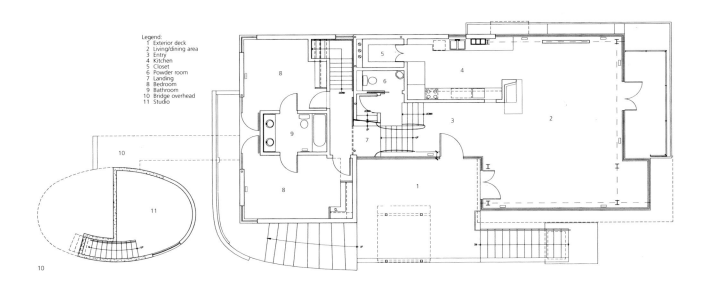

Legend:
1 Deck
2 Master bedroom
3 Master bathroom
4 Closet
5 Study
6 Bridge
7 Studio

9

Legend:
1   Exterior deck
2   Living/dining area
3   Entry
4   Kitchen
5   Closet
6   Powder room
7   Landing
8   Bedroom
9   Bathroom
10 Bridge overhead
11 Studio

10

Architect Esa Piironen

Koivikko House

Helsinki, Finland

Legend:
1 Old house
2 New annex
3 Car park

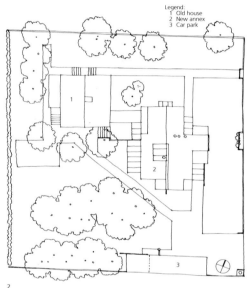

1

2

3

4

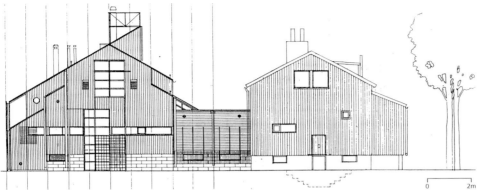

1 Courtyard
2 Site plan
3 West elevation
4 Greenhouse
5 North elevation
6 Living room
7 Fireplace detail
8 Interior detail
Photography: courtesy Arkkitehtitomisto Esa Piironen Oy

0   2m

5

7

6

8

Kronenberg Beach House

Killcare, New South Wales, Australia

1

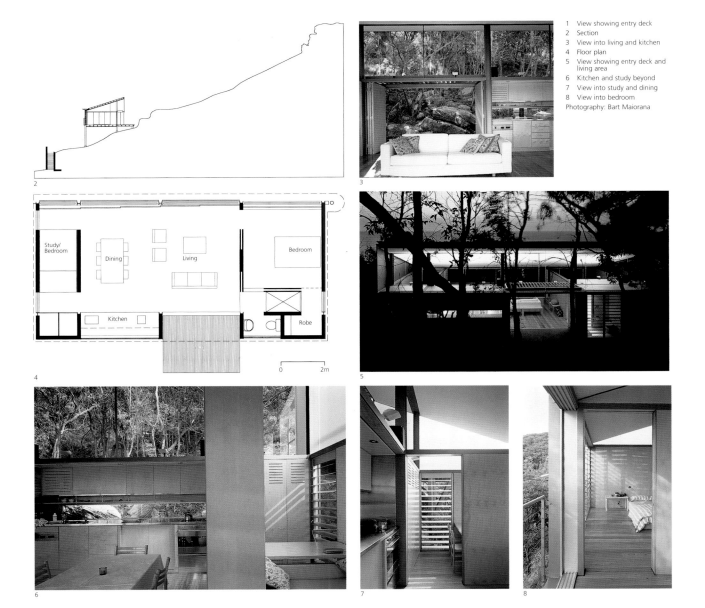

1   View showing entry deck
2   Section
3   View into living and kitchen
4   Floor plan
5   View showing entry deck and
    living area
6   Kitchen and study beyond
7   View into study and dining
8   View into bedroom
Photography: Bart Maiorana

Study/
Bedroom

Dining

Living

Bedroom

Kitchen

Robe

0   2m

Lawson-Westen House

West Los Angeles, California, USA

1

2

3

1–3   Exterior
4   Ground floor plan
5&6   Interior
7   Site plan
Photography: Tom Bonner

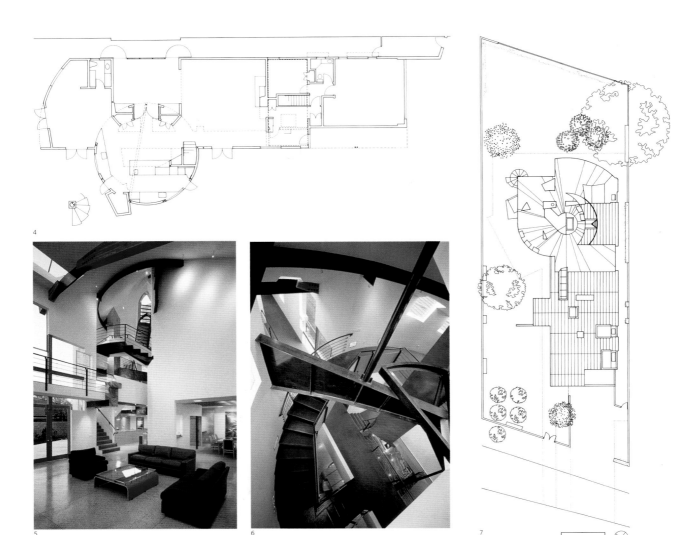

4

5

6

7

0   5m

Westwork Architects, PA

Lewton Residence

Albuquerque, New Mexico, USA

1

2

3

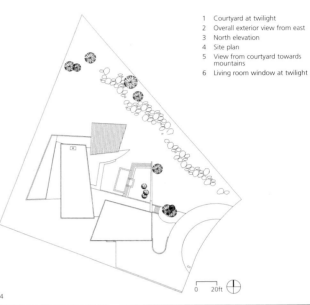

4

0   20ft

5

6

Legend:
1 Entry hall
2 Living room
3 Dining area
4 Kitchen
5 Master bedroom
6 Master bathroom
7 Office
8 Bath
9 Courtyard
10 Bedroom
11 Laundry
12 Garage
13 Reflecting pool
14 Patio

7

0   15ft

8

9

10

11

Malibu Beach House

Malibu, California, USA

1

2

3

4

5

1 Interior courtyard provides an oasis between main house and guesthouse
2 Translucent floors allow sunlight to penetrate downstairs
3 Transparent glazing ties ocean landscape to the private courtyard
4 Sculptural staircase complements owner's artistic interests
5 Concrete and teak fireplace anchors spaces in timeless and permanent manner
6 Gently curving island regulates flow from kitchen to formal dining room
7 Palette of natural materials encompasses master bedroom
8 First floor plan

Photography: Tim Street-Porter

6

7

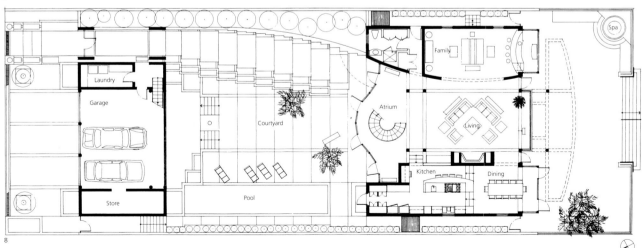

8

Malibu Residence

Malibu, California, USA

1

206

1 View from southeast
2 Site plan
3 Detail of south façade
4 North façade

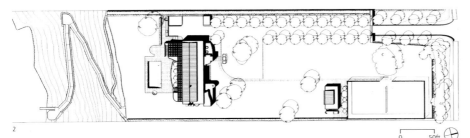

0 50ft

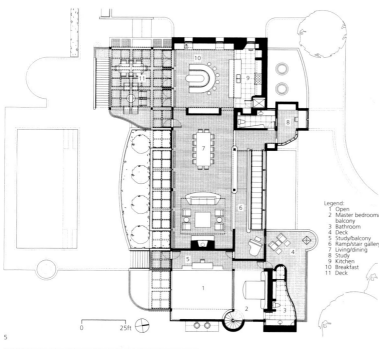

Legend:
1 Open
2 Master bedroom/
  balcony
3 Bathroom
4 Deck
5 Study/balcony
6 Ramp/stair gallery
7 Living/dining
8 Study
9 Kitchen
10 Breakfast
11 Deck

0   25ft

5

7

6

8

9

5 Main living level plan
6 Living/dining area
7 Circulation zone with exterior glazed wall
8 View of ocean from sitting room
9 Section
10 View towards dining area
Photography: Erhard Pfeiffer

10

SITE Environmental Design, Inc
Mallet House
New York, New York, USA

1

2

1   Back of house with garden patio
2   Façade of 1820's house before conversion
3   Garden view
4   Sitting room
5   Ghosted chair in living room wall
6   Ghosted bookcase installation in library
7   Ghosted equestrian equipment installation at entry hall
8   Library area to staircase
9   Ghosted clock installation on mantle piece
Photography: SITE Environmental Design, Inc. (2,5–8);
Andreas Sterzing (1,3,4); Andy Warchol (9)

The Miller/Hull Partnership, LLP

Marquand Retreat

Naches Valley, Washington, USA

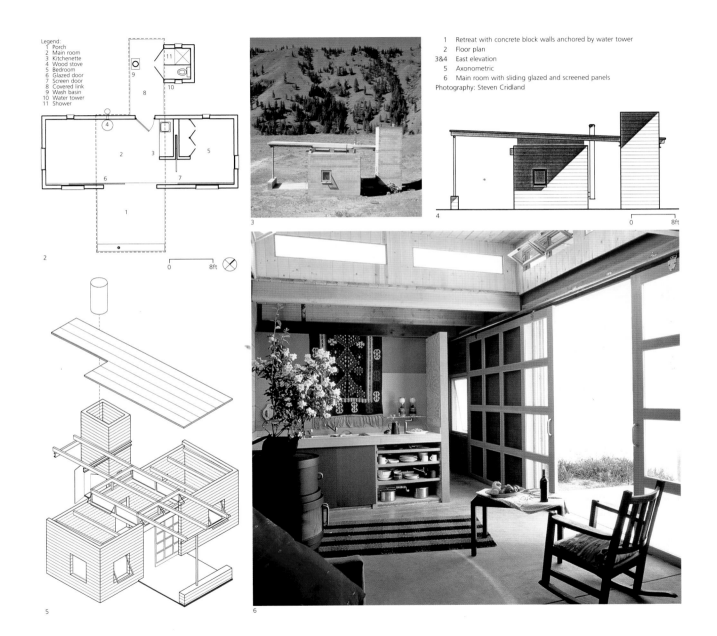

Legend:
 1 Porch
 2 Main room
 3 Kitchenette
 4 Wood stove
 5 Bedroom
 6 Glazed door
 7 Screen door
 8 Covered link
 9 Wash basin
 10 Water tower
 11 Shower

0   8ft

1 Retreat with concrete block walls anchored by water tower
2 Floor plan
3&4 East elevation
5 Axonometric
6 Main room with sliding glazed and screened panels

Photography: Steven Cridland

0   8ft

Marsh & Grochowski

Marsh House

Nottingham, UK

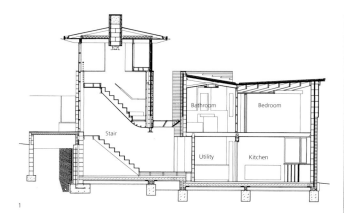

1

2

3

4

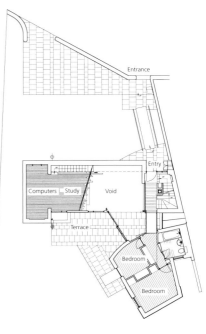

1 Section through main stairwell
2 View of house from terrace
3 View of house from south
4 View of house from road
5 Double-height living space
6 Entrance level plan
7 View of inglenook fireplace
8 Entrance balcony
9 Mezzanine studio
Photography: Andy Earl (2–5,8,9); Mark Enstone (7)

Susan A. Maxman, FAIA

Maxman Residence

Philadelphia, Pennsylvania, USA

1

1 Elevation of house facing walled garden
2 Rear garden
3 View from street
4 Rear elevation looking towards terrace and fountain

5   Living room
6   Study; original bedroom of George Howe's mother
7   Kitchen looking out to service courtyard
8   Bedroom
9   View from dining room to garden
Photography: Barry Halkin

5

6

7

8

9

Rod McAllister

Mellangoose House

Falmouth, Cornwall, UK

1

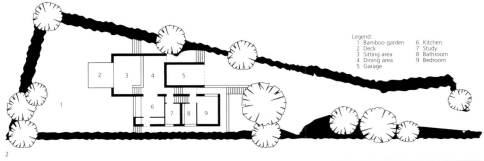

Legend:
1 Bamboo garden   6 Kitchen
2 Deck   7 Study
3 Sitting area   8 Bathroom
4 Dining area   9 Bedroom
5 Garage

1   North elevation
2   Site plan
3   Evening view from top of entrance steps at front door
4   Sitting area with dining mezzanine and kitchen beyond
5   View of top bathroom
6   Looking north towards sitting room doors
Photography: Mandy Reynolds/Fotoforum

Michaels/Sisson Residence

Mercer Island, Washington, USA

1

1   East facing entry elevation
2   Site plan
3   Section
4   Vertical house rises out of wooded ravine
5   Glass-filled steel frame opens onto private deck at rear
Photography: Fred Housel (1,4); Art Grice (5)

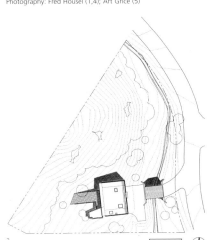

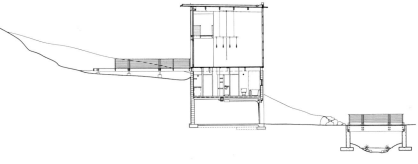

0   30ft

Moen Residence

West Des Moines, Iowa, USA

1

2

3

4

5

1 Exterior
2 Entry
3 Seating area adjacent to kitchen
4 Dining area
5 Looking towards dining area
6 Entry level floor plan
7 Lower level floor plan
8 Spaces were created to house art collection
Photography: Farshid Assassi/Assassi Productions

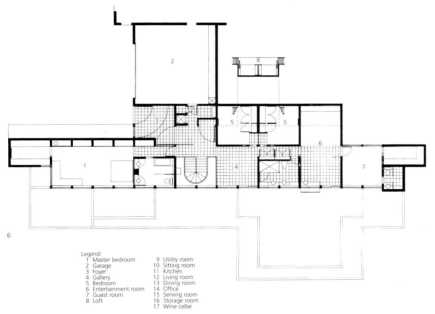

6

Legend:
1 Master bedroom
2 Garage
3 Foyer
4 Gallery
5 Bedroom
6 Entertainment room
7 Guest room
8 Loft
9 Utility room
10 Sitting room
11 Kitchen
12 Living room
13 Dining room
14 Office
15 Serving room
16 Storage room
17 Wine cellar

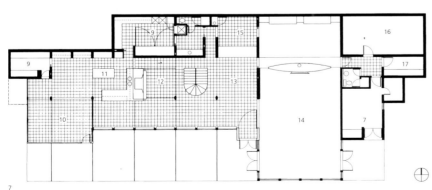

7

8

Muskoka Boathouse

Point William, Ontario, Canada

1

2

1 View from outdoor deck towards lake
2 View of exterior boat slip with outdoor deck above
3 Waterfront plan
4 View of boathouse from shoreline
5 View of boathouse from lake
6 View of lake from covered porch
7 View from covered porch

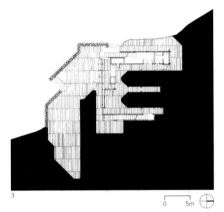

3

0   5m

4

5

6

7

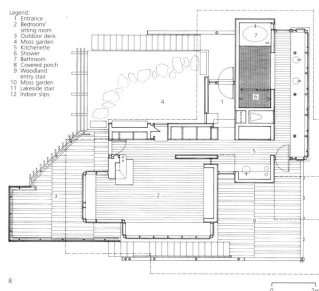

Legend:
1 Entrance
2 Bedroom/
  sitting room
3 Outdoor deck
4 Moss garden
5 Kitchenette
6 Shower
7 Bathroom
8 Covered porch
9 Woodland
  entry stair
10 Moss garden
11 Lakeside stair
12 Indoor slips

8

0   2m

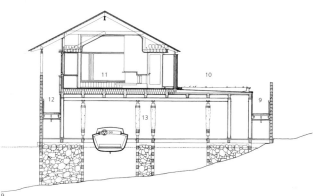

9

10

11

8   Second floor plan
9   East–west section through boathouse
10   View of bed/sitting room
11   View of bath area
12   View of bed/sitting room looking towards outdoor deck
Photography: James Dow (1,2,4,6,7,10–12); Shim Sutcliffe (5)

12

Atelier Hitoshi Abe
n-house
Kamakura, Kanagawa, Japan

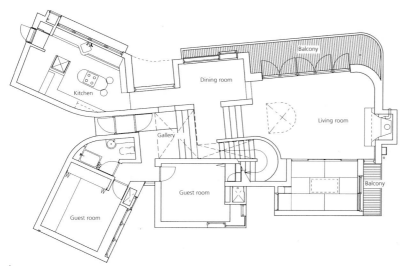

Kitchen

Dining room

Balcony

Living room

Gallery

Guest room

Balcony

Guest room

1

2

3

4

230

5

6

1 First floor plan
2 Exterior view from entry approach
3 Exterior view from south
4 Exterior view of south façade
5 View of living room and opening from stair landing

6 Kitchen
7 View up towards living room from entrance
8 Section
9 View towards living room from upper floor
Photography: NAP (2–6); Shinkenchiku-sha (7,9)

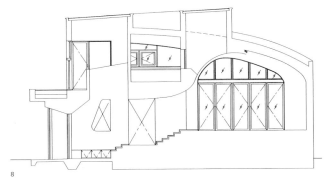

8

7

9

Nomentana Residence

Lovell, Maine, USA

1

Legend:
1 Entrance
2 Library
3 Living room
4 Dining room
5 Kitchen
6 Porch
7 Studio
8 Bedroom
9 Garage

1 Western elevation
2 Lower level plan
3 Living room porch
4 South-facing entrance

0   6m

5   East–west section facing north
6   View of living room towards deck
7   View from living room deck
8   View of entry/library/two-story impluvium
Photography: Timothy Hursley

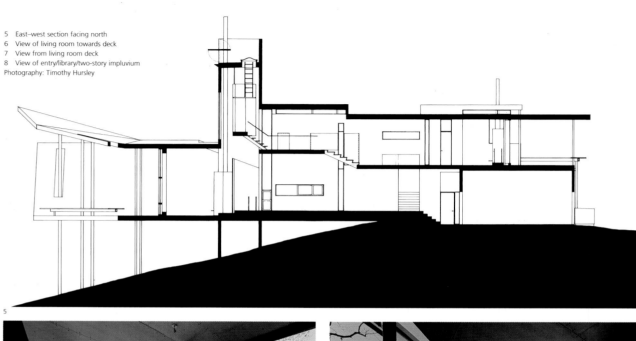

5

6

7

8

Kisho Kurokawa Architect & Associates

O Residence

Tokyo, Japan

1 Garden stream with path
2 Entrance gate
3 First floor plan
4 Outdoor bath
5 Living room
6 Garden outside tea ceremony
   room
7 Basement floor entrance
8 Tearoom corridor
Photography: Koji Kobayashi

5

6

7

8

Outside-In House

Marin County, California, USA

1

1   View of new front entry
2   View of addition at night from rear
3   Elevations (west and south)
4   View of back from pool

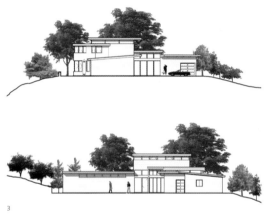

3

4

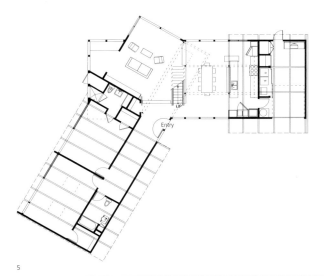

5

6

7

8

9

Photography: Matthew Millman

10

Gabriel & Elizabeth Poole Design Company

Poole Residence

Lake Weyba, Queensland, Australia

1

2

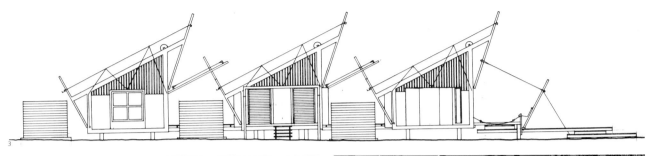

1   House from east
2   Evening shot from north
3   East elevation
4   North deck with mesh seating
5   View towards bedroom one past bath house
6   North elevation with roller door down

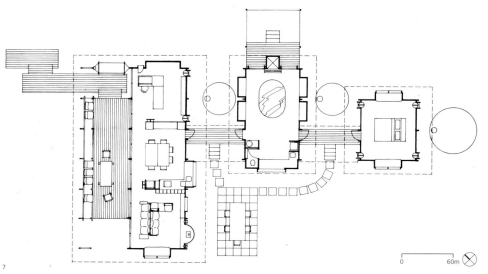

7

8

0   60m

9

10

11

Siren Architects Ltd

Puente Soivio

Vammala, Finland

1

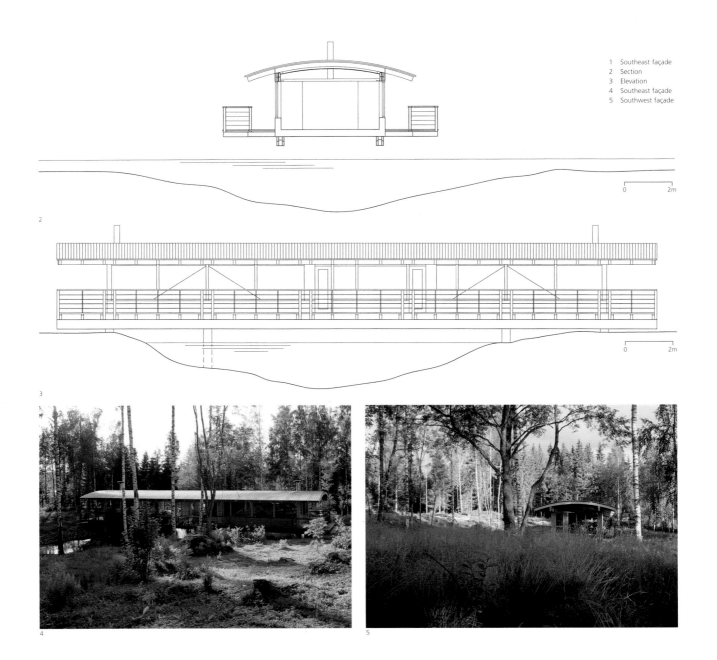

1 Southeast façade
2 Section
3 Elevation
4 Southeast façade
5 Southwest façade

0   2m

0   2m

6 Floor plan
7 Façade detail
8 Living room
9 Living room/kitchen
Photography: Lars Hallén (1,7,8);
Arno de la Chapelle (4,5,9)

Legend:
1 Living room
2 Dining room
3 Main bedroom
4 Bathroom
5 Sauna
6 Vestibule
7 Guest room

6

0   2m

7

8

9

The Cox Group
Riparian House
St Lucia, Queensland, Australia

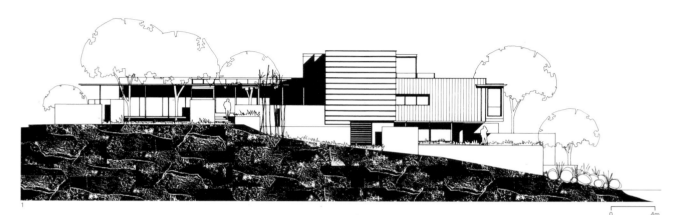

1

0   4m

2

3

1　East elevation
2　Glazing to riverfront in lowered position
3　Street entry canopy

4　View from across river
5　Zinc-clad east wall
6　Courtyard view through to river

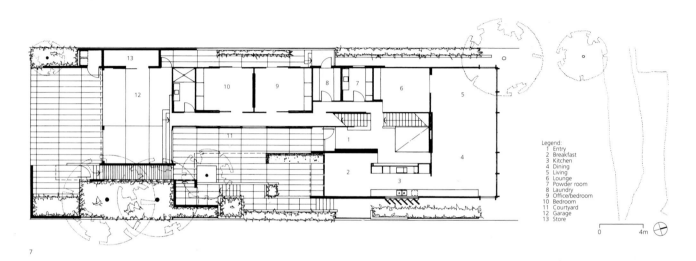

Legend:
1 Entry
2 Breakfast
3 Kitchen
4 Dining
5 Living
6 Lounge
7 Powder room
8 Laundry
9 Office/bedroom
10 Bedroom
11 Courtyard
12 Garage
13 Store

0   4m

7

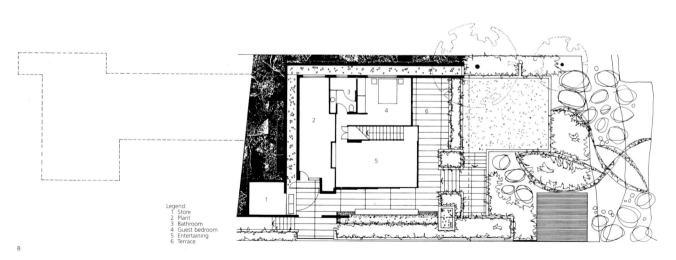

Legend:
1 Store
2 Plant
3 Bathroom
4 Guest bedroom
5 Entertaining
6 Terrace

8

9

10

7   Main (middle) level floor plan
8   Lower level floor plan
9   Living room with glazing lowered
10 Open stair to upper level
11 Entrance hall view back into courtyard
Photography: Marc Grimwald, Mark Burgin

11

T.R. Hamzah & Yeang Sdn. Bhd.

Roof-Roof House

Ampang, Selangor, Malaysia

1

1 View of house from northeast corner garden
2 Ground floor plan
3 East–west cross section
4 View of louvered roof over swimming pool
5 View of pool from north
Photography: K. L. Ng Photography

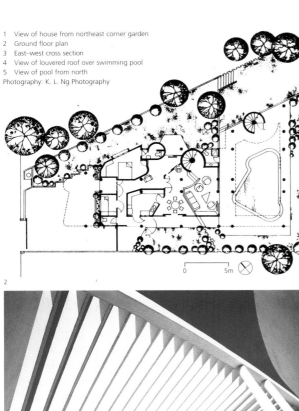

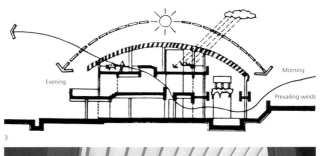

Evening

Morning

Prevailing winds

3

4

5

Roth Residence

Oakland, California, USA

1

1 Street-facing block
2 Three blocks are finished in cedar plywood and lumber, integrally colored stucco, and copper-faced shingles
3 Floor plan
4 One block is fashioned in stained cedar boards and plywood

5 Bedroom with fireplace finished in metallic copper ceramic tiles
6 Fireplace inglenook is a miniature of the house's street-facing block

Photography: Alan Weintraub

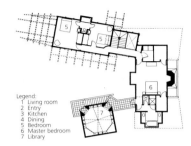

Legend:
1 Living room
2 Entry
3 Kitchen
4 Dining
5 Bedroom
6 Master bedroom
7 Library

2

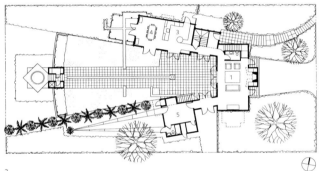

3

4

5

6

Rotunda House

Nichada Thani Village, Nothaburi, Thailand

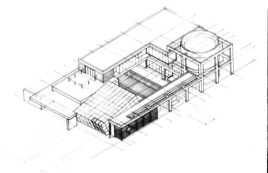

Roxbury Drive Residence

Beverly Hills, California, USA

1

2

1 Section
2 Architecturally defined curves and lines are displayed throughout house
3 Pool has an internal wall dividing shallow and deep ends
4 Floor plan
5 Staircase leads to second level with its curved walls, and display of artwork and sculptural pieces
6 Interior and exterior are connected through floor-to-ceiling glass walls that slide into pockets and offer a view of reflecting pool and artwork centerpiece

Photography: Maria Antonia Viteri

3

4

Legend:
1 Breakfast room
2 Butler's pantry
3 Family room
4 Formal dining room
5 Formal living room
6 Front entry
7 Garage
8 Kitchen
9 Laundry
10 Maid's room
11 Reflecting room

5

6

Ray Kappe, FAIA

Shapiro Residence

Santa Monica Canyon, California, USA

1 Entrance stair to gallery
2 Dining room deck at canyon
3 Axonometric
4 Gallery and living room from second floor

3

4

5

6

7

8

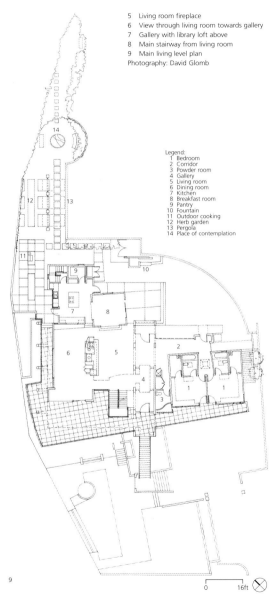

9

5 Living room fireplace
6 View through living room towards gallery
7 Gallery with library loft above
8 Main stairway from living room
9 Main living level plan
Photography: David Glomb

Legend:
1 Bedroom
2 Corridor
3 Powder room
4 Gallery
5 Living room
6 Dining room
7 Kitchen
8 Breakfast room
9 Pantry
10 Fountain
11 Outdoor cooking
12 Herb garden
13 Pergola
14 Place of contemplation

0   16ft

Graham Phillips, Architect
Skywood House
Middlesex, UK

1

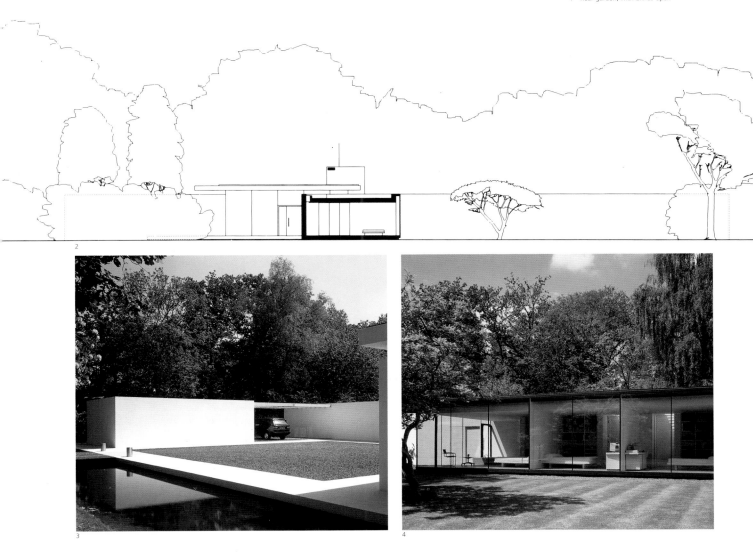

1 Daytime view of front elevation across lake
2 Section
3 Courtyard with car
4 Rear garden, with blinds open

2

3

4

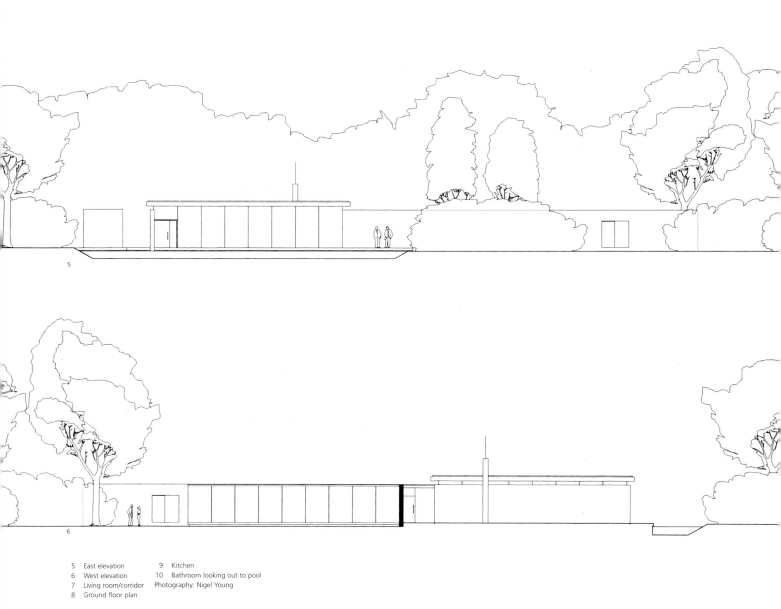

5   East elevation   9   Kitchen
6   West elevation   10   Bathroom looking out to pool
7   Living room/corridor   Photography: Nigel Young
8   Ground floor plan

Legend:
1 Entry
2 Living
3 Dining
4 Kitchen
5 Utility
6 Cloakroom
7 Bedroom
8 Garage/studio
9 Pool

A Water
B Gravel
C Lawn

0   10m

McIntosh Poris Associates

Sloan Residence

Bloomington Hills, Michigan, USA

1 Two-story house is designed in relationship to its landscape, which overlooks Long Lake and Island Lake in Bloomington Hills

2 Glass windows were incorporated into design to appreciate outdoor landscape view and lakes

3 Interior elements are delineated in mahogany wood to soften the design and emphasize strength of landscape

4 Kitchen features stainless steel and verde marble with custom-made rice paper-backed windowed cabinets

5 Bedroom is oriented to look out into outdoor scenery through glass windows and doors

Photography: Balthazar Korab

2

3

4

5

Barry A. Berkus, AIA

Terner Residence and Entenza Remodel

Pacific Palisades, California, USA

1

2

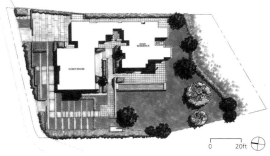

3

4

1   Modernism references cubism in the Terner Residence

2   A juxtaposition of old and new: the Eames Case Study House #9 and the newly built Terner Residence

3   Site Plan

4   Colors and geometry inspired by Eames mark the entrance

5

6

7

8

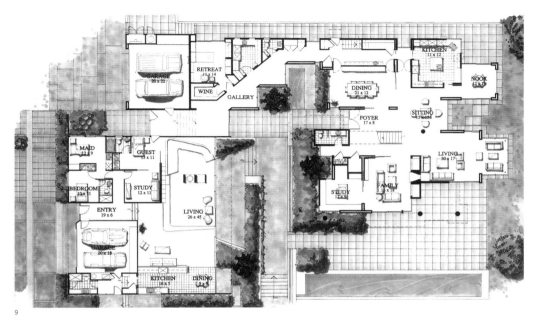

5&6 Shoji screens allow for flexible
     space in the Terner Residence

7   Interiors by Dana Berkus

8   Mid-century modern furniture
     is consistent with the Eames
     design

9   First floor, Terner Residence

10   Second floor, Terner Residence

11   View towards the third-story
     office

Photography: Tom Bonner

9

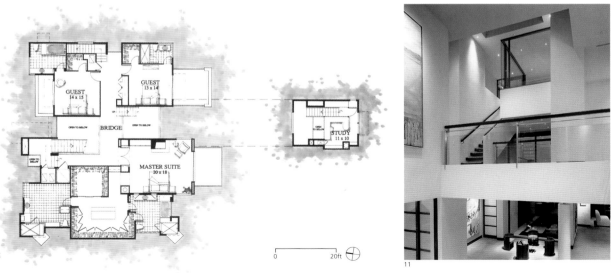

10

0   20ft

11

Bohlin Cywinski Jackson

The Ledge House

Catoctin Mountains, Maryland, USA

1

2

3

4

Photography: Karl Backus, AIA

5

Legend:
1 Master bedroom
2 Study
3 Living space
4 Kitchen
5 Screened porch
6 Bedroom
7 Bedroom
8 Pool
9 Mechanical
10 Entrance

Tree House

Balmoral, Sydney, Australia

1

1 Assembly in steel and glass nestled into lush terrain
2 Entry and diffused glass stair 'box'
3 Glazed walls viewing directly into bush
4 Cross section down rocky terrain
5 South façade
6 Timber decks fan out to sun and views from living and bedrooms

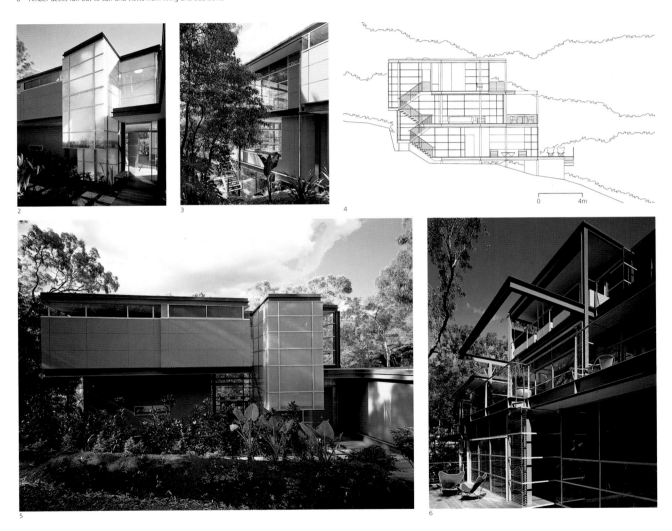

2

3

4

0   4m

5

6

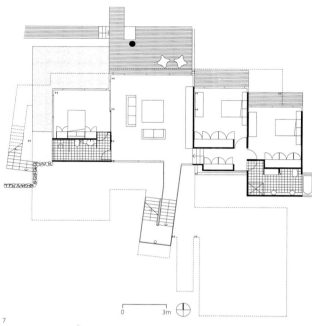

7   Lower level plan
8   Living, dining, and sun room pavilion
9   Open-tread staircase in diffused glass "box"
10 Entry and stair
11 Kitchen and family/sun room

Photography: Ross Honeysett

9

8

10

Nagle Hartray Danker Kagan McKay Architects Planners
Trillium Springs Farmhouse
New Buffalo, Michigan, USA

1

1 Sunset view of south façade from pond
2 Entry level plan
3 View of porte cochere connecting main
   house to garage/farm office
4 View of southwest corner with guest house
   in foreground
5 View from entry drive

Legend:
1 Office
2 Garage
3 Breakfast room
4 Kitchen/dining room
5 Family room
6 Living room
7 Screened porch
8 Guest house

0   16ft

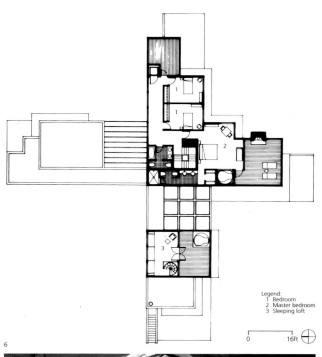

6

7

Legend:
1 Bedroom
2 Master bedroom
3 Sleeping loft

0   16ft

8

9

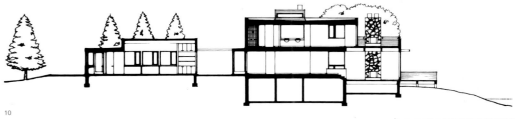

10

6   Upper level plan
7   View of walkway with sunscreen
8   View of guest quarters
9   View from kitchen to dining area
10 Building section
11 Kitchen
Photography: Bruce Van Inwegen

11

Trillium Springs Farmhouse **291**

Turtle Creek House

Dallas, Texas, USA

1

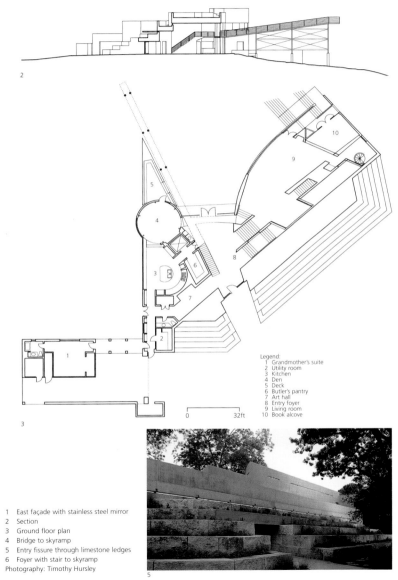

2

3

Legend:
1 Grandmother's suite
2 Utility room
3 Kitchen
4 Den
5 Deck
6 Butler's pantry
7 Art hall
8 Entry foyer
9 Living room
10 Book alcove

0   32ft

4

6

1 East façade with stainless steel mirror
2 Section
3 Ground floor plan
4 Bridge to skyramp
5 Entry fissure through limestone ledges
6 Foyer with stair to skyramp
Photography: Timothy Hursley

5

Turtle Creek House **293**

Tyler Residence

Tubac, Arizona, USA

1

1 Main living space and courtyard open
   up over negative-edge pool to distant
   mountain vistas
2 Three hovering and glowing forms
   signal approach
3 Floor plan

4 Southeast façade is accentuated by oxidized
   plate steel boxes, which serve as both
   window frames and shades
5 Courtyard serves as artificial oasis where
   one can escape to the smell of sage and
   gentle sounds of trickling water

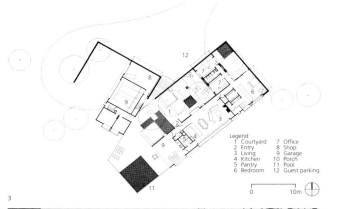

3

Legend:
1 Courtyard   7 Office
2 Entry   8 Shop
3 Living   9 Garage
4 Kitchen   10 Porch
5 Pantry   11 Pool
6 Bedroom   12 Guest parking

0   10m

2

4

5

6

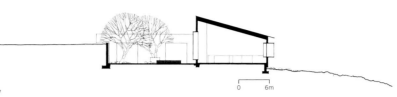

7

8

9

6   Materials cross in bedroom, carrying
    outside in and inside out
7   Section
8   Corridor through house allows a
    continuous undisturbed view

9   Ten-foot-square dining area window
    connects main living space to courtyard
10 View along 35-foot-long main living space
    window provides a glimpse of natural
    surroundings
Photography: Bill Timmerman

10

Shubin + Donaldson Architects

Urban Residence

Laguna Beach, California, USA

1

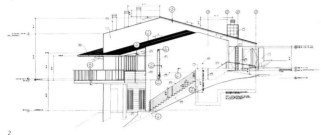

1 House was designed to overlook ocean view from virtually every room
2 Sectional view of house illustrates layout of rooms
3 Kitchen was designed to take advantage of views of ocean and coast
4 Living room area is angled to overlook bay view and enable cool breezes to enter
5 Natural light comes in through skylight and windows to brighten up entry hall and stairwell in living room area

Photography: Farshid Assassi and Peter Malinowski

7 View from terrace
8 Kitchen
9 South elevation
10 Children's bedroom
11 Longitudinal section
12 Cross section
13 Bridge over void of sitting room
   with stairs to first floor
14 Sitting room
Photography: N. Danielides

9

7

8

10

11

12

0   5m

13

14

Villa le Goff

Marseille, France

1

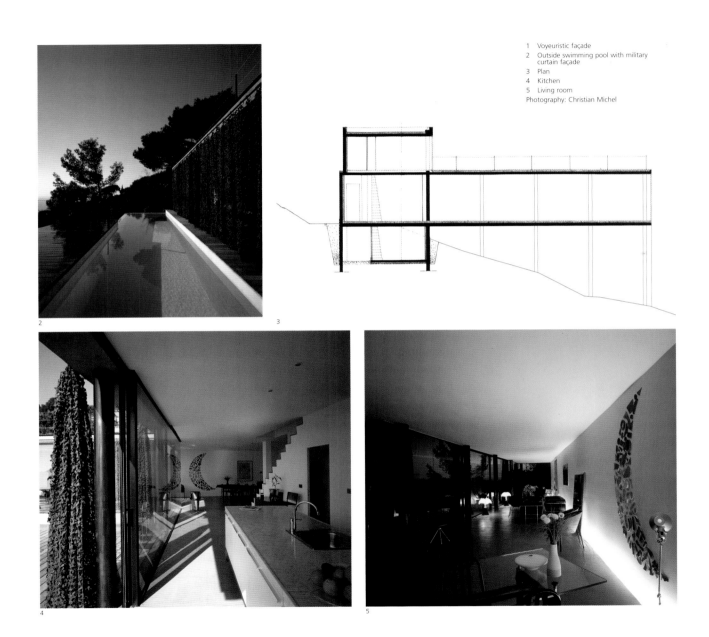

1 Voyeuristic façade
2 Outside swimming pool with military curtain façade
3 Plan
4 Kitchen
5 Living room
Photography: Christian Michel

Villa te Goes

Goes, Netherlands

1

1 South façade
2 West façade
3 Site plan
4 View from dining room
5 Dining room

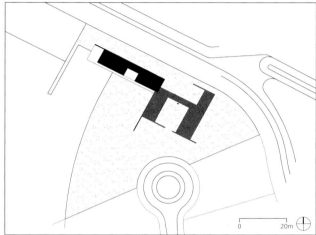

0　　　　20m

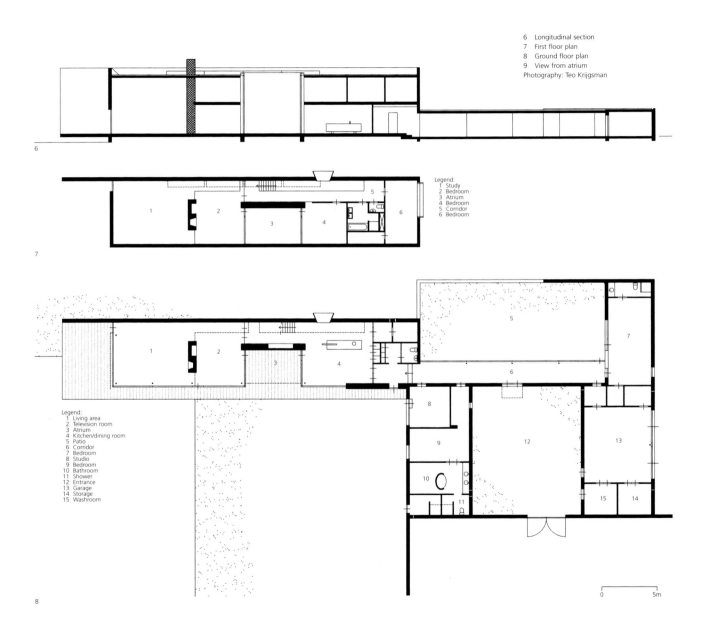

6 Longitudinal section
7 First floor plan
8 Ground floor plan
9 View from atrium
Photography: Teo Krijgsman

6

Legend:
1 Study
2 Bedroom
3 Atrium
4 Bedroom
5 Corridor
6 Bedroom

7

Legend:
1 Living area
2 Television room
3 Atrium
4 Kitchen/dining room
5 Patio
6 Corridor
7 Bedroom
8 Studio
9 Bedroom
10 Bathroom
11 Shower
12 Entrance
13 Garage
14 Storage
15 Washroom

8

0   5m

9

Wakeham House

Rogate, West Sussex, UK

1

9

Charles Rose Architects Inc.

West 22nd Street Residence

Chelsea, New York, USA

1

1   View of central courtyard
2   Double-story gallery elevation
3   Elevation
4   Section
5   View of upper terrace looking north
6   View from gallery towards children's bedrooms

2

3

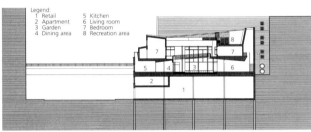

Legend:
1 Retail   5 Kitchen
2 Apartment   6 Living room
3 Garden   7 Bedroom
4 Dining area   8 Recreation area

4

5

6

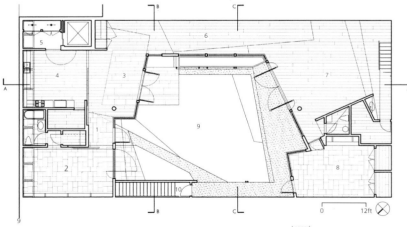

7

8

9

10

7   Dining room with kitchen beyond
8   Living room
9   Third floor plan
10 View of stair hall at bedroom level
11 View from lower gallery to living room
Photography: Chuck Choi Photography,
Architectural Photography

Legend:
1 Foyer   6 Gallery
2 Study   7 Living room
3 Dining area   8 Family room
4 Kitchen   9 Garden
5 Mudroom   10 Entry vestibule

0   12ft

11

Yudell-Beebe House

Sea Ranch, California, USA

1 House feathers into landscape by its articulation, scale, and material palette

2 On meadow side the roof slopes towards the land, while bays frame views to sea

3 Site plan articulates a hierarchy of places and courts, which respond to diverse site and environmental orientations

4 Street façades present a strongly geometric contemporary interpretation of the "western" front

5 House both merges towards land with low bays and marks its place with study "towers"

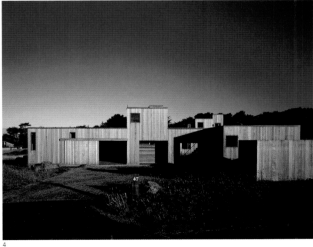

2

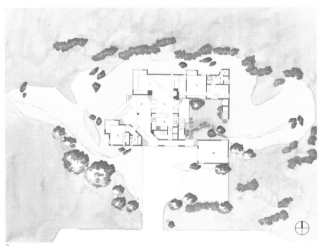

3

4

5

Legend:
1 Living room
2 Dining room
3 Master bedroom
4 Master bathroom
5 Porch
6 Guest room
7 Guest bathroom
8 Kitchen
9 Garden court
10 Garage
11 Closet
12 Laundry
13 Guest parking

0   10ft

6

7

8

9

10

11th & Hill Residence

Santa Monica, California, USA
Trout Studios

Client: Sallie Trout and family
House area: 2,400 square feet/223 square meters
Site area: 6,000 square feet/557 square meters
Materials: Dryvit exterior, cement, plaster, sandstone, bamboo flooring, lead sheeting, bluestone, Baltic birch, ribbed glass

From the exterior, a striking deep-blue color and multiple metal roofline sets the stage for a playful and unusual design. Dryvit, a color-impregnated cement-like material, clads the building; its brilliant color is stable so that no repainting will be necessary. Low cement walls with custom-designed redwood-and-steel fencing enclose the landscaping of Mexican weeping bamboo, lavender, rosemary, flax, chamomile, sage, and jasmine. Cement walk is accented with blue glass marbles and cast-iron brad-point stars.

Interior rooms are delineated more by changes in flooring materials than by constructed walls. Bamboo flooring defines the living room, home office, and den, while raised-coin, non-PVC rubber resilient flooring is set in a curved pattern in the kitchen and dining areas.

A large curved wall with lighted niches displays a collection of art pottery. Other collections accommodated by design include cast-iron toys, guitars, sculptures, and photography.

Alumbrera

Mustique, St. Vincent and the Grenadines, West Indies
A.J. Diamond, Donald Schmitt and Company

House area: 10,000 square feet/929 square meters
Site area: 5.5 acres/2.2 hectares
Materials: White cedar, greenheart (Guyana), ipe (Brazil), concrete, cement, stucco, mahogany, glass mosaic tiles

Alumbrera is located on Mustique, a privately owned island in the Grenadines, West Indies. The 1,800-acre (728-hectare) island has been developed as one of the world's most exclusive resorts, and when fully developed will have no more than 100 villas and a small hotel.

The residence is a five-bedroom complex covering 10,000 square feet (929 square meters). It is organized as a series of smaller pavilions and recreational facilities, linked by landscaped gardens and terraces, arranged to take advantage of the views and prevailing winds on the large hilltop site. Separate components include the living pavilion with large areas for dining and entertaining, bedroom pavilion, guest suite pavilion, and kitchen pavilion, all arranged around a central terrace. Site components include a carport, staff cottage, swimming pool, beach access stair, and tennis courts.

The residence takes full advantage of its beautiful site, allowing for an open-air lifestyle while providing luxurious seclusion and privacy.

Ambrosini/Neu Residence

Los Angeles, California, USA
Kanner Architects

House area: 3,500 square feet/325 square meters
Site area: 4,500 square feet/418 square meters
Materials: Steel moment frames and wood framing, cement plaster stucco, ceramic mosaic tile, stone veneer, aluminum storefront system with Douglas fir wood operable windows and doors

Timeless, functional, affordable, modernist, and warm—these were the clients' most important requirements for their new home in Los Angeles. The clients themselves are a professional couple in their 50s without children, who both love music and have concerts in their home.

The small two-story structure responds to a long list of functional issues: street orientation, views to the hillside at the back, lighting, privacy, acoustics, love of cooking, and budget. Aesthetically, it is influenced by a number of modernist and case study homes located nearby.

Large expanses of glass, which are unseen from the street, allow each room a view of the hills and the ravine beyond. The L-shaped plan is rotated on the site in order to obtain optimal views and increase the south sideyard adjacent to the lower bedroom. The street façade is intentionally long, sculptural, and opaque. This helps mitigate road noise and creates privacy.

The main goal was to create a restrained modernist design that responds to its canyon setting. A two-story living room that acoustically doubles as a mini concert hall and wide outdoor sleeping decks make the home more flexible.

Art House

London, UK
Brookes Stacey Randall, Architects

House area: 4,854 square feet/451 square meters
Site area: 5,651 square feet/525 square meters

When the client purchased the property it was in very poor condition and needed extensive remedial work and modification to achieve his brief. This included total demolition of the interior, underpinning, the lowering of the ground floor, and creation of new basements.

The design sought to maximize the sense of space, using a palette of materials and colors that are uplifting and welcoming. The house is accessed by a discreet entrance from the street which provides no sense of the scale of the place beyond. From the entrance area a guest is led into the gallery, which is a triple-height space designed for the display of works of art.

Turning the corner one becomes aware how the space flows into the central volume that is the social heart of the home. The design includes carefully designed visual diagonals to reveal the greatest possible sense of space at particular points. The two courtyards are visible from this "living room" and the large format French limestone runs throughout, separated only by opening glass walls. During clement weather the glass walls fold away to provide uninhibited access and enjoyment of the complete site. A suspended chimney of red polished plaster hangs above the living space. This chimney has no apparent means of support as it has been suspended from the roof structure, creating views through the flames of the fire.

Art-Nouveau Villa

Sacro Monte, Varese, Italy
SPATIUM

House area: 9,332 square feet/867 square meters
Site area: 52,744 square feet/4,900 square meters
Materials: Granite columns, pebble-stone, black and white marble, mosaic, oak and walnut parquet, stucco, painted canvas

This villa, dated 1901, is located in the neighborhood of Varese, in the hills of Sacro Monte, a place that was once a holiday resort and spa. At the end of the 1980s, its restoration was only half finished and was aimed at reconciling the art-nouveau style of the building with the rational rigor of the modern movement. For the interiors geometrical grid patterns with black and white contrasts were chosen, easily recognizable as citations from Josef Hoffmann.

Ten years later, the new restoration and interior design have been completed, doubling the living space of the old residence. At first glance a contrasting impression can be made, depending on the viewpoint. The original space was and still is rarefied and aims to lead the attention towards the exterior. On the contrary, the new space reverses this perspective and brings the landscape inside the home. The "winter" living room, with its frescoed walls, contrasts the older "summer" room, which is much barer. A feature of the new restoration is a trompe-l'oeil composition representing a fence of pilasters decorated with pomegranates, through which one can view the distant landscape.

Baan Kamonorrathep

Rimtai Saitarn, Mae Rim District, Chiang Mai, Thailand
Architects 49

Interior design by owner
Client: Khun Chairat Kamonorrathep
House area: 2,637 square feet/245 square meters
Materials: Reinforced concrete, polished cement, wood and plastered brick walls, wooden shingle roof

This weekender recreational home for a newly wedded couple with no children is located 20 kilometers (12.4 miles) from the center of the ancient city of Chiang-Mai, on a hillside surrounded by mountains and a natural stream.

The design is traditional both in its arrangement and appearance. The layout is simple, clean, and well suited to relaxation. The architecture, interior, and landscape harmonize with the surroundings, which include many traditional Thai dwellings. The overlapping roof signifies the vernacular appeal of the house.

The house has effective ventilation suitable for tropical architecture, incorporating shades to deflect direct sunlight and heat, and protect from rain. The use of materials includes traditional local products, such as teak for the shingle roof, column, ceiling, doors, and windows, with some terracotta wall tiles.

The plan is generally typical of north-Thailand houses, which have a pool at the heart of the house. The guestroom is an altered rice barn, and the recreation space from a traditional pavilion. The best views from the house are from the rear of the block, where the living room, multipurpose area, and pool have been located, to breath fresh air and enjoy splendid views of the rice fields and the surrounding mountains.

Bartlit Residence

Castle Pines, Colorado, USA
Lake/Flato Architects, Inc.

House area: 6,500 square feet/604 square meters
Site area: 2.63 acres/1 hectare
Materials: Lightweight steel frame, Native Empire stone, gunnison granite, Colorado sandstone, polished plaster walls and ceilings, copper and oak ceilings, copper roof and walls, White Oak cabinetry and floors

The design creates a series of varied living spaces that follow the contours of the site and are connected by a north–south gallery that runs along the edge of the ridge. The east-facing guest bedrooms are dug into the slope, covered by earthen roofs, open to sunlit courtyards and atriums. West-facing public pavilions perch boldly on the steep site, their soaring roofs and expanses of glass affording sweeping views. At the gallery's north end, the master suite was designed to operate as a separate wing, creating privacy and an intimate scale for the owners.

The dialogue between stone, steel, and glass, roots the house firmly in the land and blurs the division between inside and out. To reinforce this relationship, a series of carefully detailed openings—courtyards, atriums, and windows—provide glimpses of the surroundings. This connection culminates in an outdoor arbor with stone floors that flow without thresholds from the gallery out through large glass pocket doors.

The site's development was conceived as a series of outdoor and indoor spaces that flow down the slope beginning at the entry approach, continuing through the house, and out again through the arbor. From there, steps lead down to the fire pit, then wind down the slope to a grotto adjacent to the rock quarry pool.

Beach House

Long Beach Island, New Jersey, USA
Brian Healy Architects and Michael Ryan Architects

Long Beach Island is a thin barrier island along the central coast of New Jersey used primarily as a summer resort. The site is located on the Atlantic Ocean along the northern edge of the island at a natural curve of the beach offering distant views to the north. The parcel is located at the end of a small lane adjacent to a popular walkway across the dunes to the beach.

Like much of the island, the street is as influential as the beach in shaping the experience of the place. The house challenges the autonomy of adjacent homes by acknowledging and reinforcing the collective edges of the street and waterfront. In the process, the building mediates between the vertical wall of the street and the strong horizontal presence of the ocean. The building is dependent on its relationship to this landscape, the articulation of building components, and use of color with its temporal effects and natural sympathies to the site.

At the end of the street, the building extends in a civic gesture to engage the street. In doing so it creates a public drop-off bench at the entrance to the beach. The house maintains a reserved presence along the street while the building opens itself up to views along the coast.

A glass pavilion contains the primary social spaces with the main bedroom located on the upper level. Guest quarters and secondary bedrooms are congregated in a separate wing or "motel." The main living area was raised above-grade to take advantage of the views and breezes. Wooden slats provide solar protection from the morning sun.

Beckhard House

Glen Cove, New York, USA
Herbert Beckhard Franck Richlan & Associates

Client: Elanor and Herbert Beckhard
House area: 2,800 square feet/260 square meters
Site area: 1 acre/0.4 hectares
Materials: Bluestone flooring, unfinished cypress board ceilings and walls, fieldstone fireplace wall and gypsum board walls, fieldstone walls, glass, cypress siding, painted board and batten wood siding, tar and gravel roof

Existing specimen trees were the principal factor in determining the plan of this house Herbert Beckhard designed for his own family. Beckhard preserved six spectacular trees on the site by weaving the plan into the spaces between them. Freestanding exterior fieldstone walls at the front and rear of the house are in concert with the surrounding natural landscape. The walls articulate the stone's many subtle hues, rugged textures, and distinctive shapes. They provide privacy and create outdoor "rooms" including an entry court.

Large expanses of floor-to-ceiling glass visually extend the interior space to include the courtyards and garden. The living room embraces the entry courtyard, in effect another room in itself. Toward the rear, or south, a low stone retaining wall, some 12 feet (3.6 meters) beyond the glass, defines the space beyond the living and dining rooms. A higher exterior wall at the rear provides privacy for the master bedroom, which adjoins the living room.

The use of natural materials inside the house further emphasizes the dialog between interior and exterior. A dramatic fieldstone wall/fireplace separates the living room, dining area, and kitchen. Principal interior areas feature ceilings and many walls of unfinished honey-colored cypress boards and floors of natural cleft bluestone.

The house is divided into three zones. The master bedroom suite, living room, dining room and kitchen comprise the first. A separate children's wing to the east, the second zone, contains bedrooms of four children and a separate children's living room. Each child's room has a floor-to-ceiling sliding glass window providing direct access to the outdoors. The third zone is a garage with attached guest quarters.

Bordeaux House

Bordeaux, France
Rem Koolhaas, Office of Metropolitan Architecture

House area: 5,382 square feet/500 square meters
Materials: Concrete, steel, aluminum, glass

This house was specifically designed to accommodate a wheelchair-bound husband and his wife. The couple purchased land on a mountain with panoramic city views, and instructed the architect to design a complex house rather than a simple house to define the husband's world.

The architect designed a house that is really three houses on top of each other. The lowest is a series of caverns carved from a hill for intimate family life. The highest level is divided into an area for the couple and one for their children. The most important level is a glass room sandwiched in the middle—half inside and half outside—which is almost invisible.

The husband has his own room or station, with a lift 9.8 feet by 11.6 feet (3 meters by 3.5 meters) that moves between the three levels, changing the plan and function with each movement between the floors. A single wall next to the elevator intersects each floor and contains everything the husband might need—books, artwork, and wine from the cellar.

The elevator is the heart of the house with each movement changing the architecture.

Brick Bay House

Warkworth, New Zealand
Noel Lane Architects

Principal Architect: Noel Lane
Project Team: Derek Dismeyer, Mike Farrant, Michael Pepper, Simon Twose, Nicholas Stevens

The Brick Bay House is situated within a large farm setting an hour's drive north of Auckland; the spectacular landscape hangs on the edge of sea and sky overlooking the Pacific Ocean. The house and its vast surroundings create a scene that mirrors the passage of a vessel on the undulating surface of the ocean.

The house sits on the site in heroic fashion, with a rigidity almost complete—the sea, some 200 meters (656 feet) away, is kept at bay—while turning its back to the scenic play of the landscape as if in a state of departure from its own surroundings. But once inside, the land and sea appear to be constructed and revealed around its bulk, gathering and holding them for the occupants to experience.

The rendered tapering perimeter walls mimic the solidity and mass of masonry walls. Like the roof, the walls are separate elements that function to convey the idea of a dwelling rather than propose the structure of a dwelling. These operate more like screens rather than solid elements which divide space.

The house interior mimics a playful outdoor nature with a series of containers distributed vertically and connected by walkways, bridges, and ladders. These transitional devices break up volume and space, reinforcing its component-like nature. Basic dwelling elements have been taken apart and refashioned into identities in their own right: the re-assembly results in a convoluted interior. Furthermore, they enable the house to be viewed from a continually shifting point, fragmenting the viewer's experience, so that the house becomes a collection of constructed views and scenes to be seen from the kinetic perspective of the occupant.

Brody House

Star Island, Miami Beach, Florida, USA
Singer Architects

House area: 8,800 square feet/817 square meters
Site area: 40,000 square feet/3,716 square meters

With only 26 homesites, this small island at the eastern end of the MacArthur Causeway, which connects Miami Beach to mainland Miami, has long been the most special of special places overlooking the skyline of the city. The island has been home to mobsters, royalty, sports personalities, and entertainers and still carries with it the glamour of the unapproachable.

The major goal of the design became the provision of visual access to the views of Biscayne Bay and the Miami skyline. The plan is a direct accommodation to that task and grows out of an early diagram, which used a 24-foot square (2.2 square meters) to create a series of interlocking spatial entities.

The diagram created an axis at 45 degrees to the east–west axis of the site establishing an interaction between angular and rectangular geometries. The space interconnects vertically as well, using alternating courses of gray and tan block, creating an informal environment in which spatial relationships are three dimensional. The spatial extension created by the drama of the site is an active part of the sculptural aspect of the space.

Brooke Coombes House

London, UK
Burd Haward Marston Architects

Client: John Brooke and Carol Coombes
House area: 2,153 square feet/200 square meters

This design is an innovative, simple, and modern family house that was buildable by the client, but that was not limited by commonly understood "self build" methods or materials of construction and the resulting low-tech aesthetic. The goal was to make use of available specialist technology rather than handicraft tradition.

The design also explored an economical yet expansive model of (sub)urban family living, one which engaged with contemporary issues of sustainability and energy conservation, whilst at the same time responding to the very particular surroundings—a suburban conservation area in West London.

The traditional front/back relationship of the suburban house is subverted by placing the living accommodation in an economical narrow strip to one side of the site. Instead of a front and back garden, a continuous garden strip runs from the street, through the house to the rear garden. Where it passes inside the house, the strip becomes a double-height glazed courtyard space. The result of this is that the main view from the house is to the side—into the courtyard. This courtyard acts as a transitory space, mediating between private/public and inside/outside activity.

Brouwer House

Gauteng, South Africa
Adrian Maserow Architects

"Kgotla" by Lemaseya Khama
House area: 7,179 square feet/667 square meters
Site area: 22,960 square feet/2,133 square meters

The context of this two-level brick and glass highveld home is earth, water, and sky. The symmetrical posture of the house uses a geometry which opens axially along the entry pool/vista in both the horizontal and vertical planes.

The courtyard is lined by terraces on either side to provide shade from the African sun. The living space is located on the ground floor, with the bedrooms on the first floor. The volumes are expansive in the house, with the staircase penetrating the double volume. Simple planes and uncluttered niches are carved into thick paneled masonry walls, contrasting with the choice of lightweight materials, which creates a living space characterized by luminosity and elegance.

Buckwalter House

Lancaster, Pennsylvania, USA
Hugh Newell Jacobsen, FAIA

The "telescope house" was common to eastern Pennsylvania, especially in the utopian communities that existed there more than a century ago. Increments were gradually added as families grew, with each successive addition made to the gable end of its predecessor, repeating the proportions but reducing the size.

The design of this house abstracts 18th- and 19th-century "telescope" traditions. Each of the seven units descends in height and diminishes in width in regular reductions of two feet on each side. This reduction in size permitted the fitting of mirrored, insulating glass in the exposed walls of each of the adjoining larger units. The reflective quality of the glass allows daytime privacy and conserves energy; the glass surrounds also admit natural light and provide surprising glimpses of the out-of-doors.

Each unit of the house reflects a specific use: living room; three-story entry foyer and circulation; library/dining room; kitchen; laundry/mudroom; and workshop. Each pavilion is an individual structure.

Buena Vista Park Residence

San Francisco, California, USA
Inglese Architecture

House area: 2,920 square feet/271 square meters
Site area: 1,875 square feet/174 square meters
Materials: Concrete, steel, cement plaster, aluminum, maple, stainless steel, glass mosaic tiles

The clients, a young professional couple, both have design backgrounds and non-traditional building aspirations. The requested design guides were order, clarity, light, and volume. Design discussion referred to the building in terms of a living being with a face, skeleton of steel, organs, and skin.

As with all major residential construction in San Francisco, an involved process of neighborhood notification and consultation was followed during design development. An existing two-story bungalow was removed, which required additional neighborhood review.

The residence has three sleeping spaces, two bathrooms, a powder room, laundry, and voluminous living/kitchen space. In addition, a roof terrace, back terrace, and a two-car garage were included. The building revels in volume, gestures towards the views, and creates a feeling of movement through the site.

Burns Residence

Venice, California, USA
Glen Irani Architects

House area: 2,900 square feet/269 square meters
Site area: 2,850 square feet/265 square meters
Materials: Exposed concrete, cement plaster, steel, aluminum, glass, cherry and maple wood millwork

Sited on a south-facing, canal-fronting lot, this two-story house contains 2,900 square feet (269 square meters) of living area. As is typical of the neighborhood's rowhouse-like concept, the 30-foot-high (9-meter) structure is on a 30 by 95-foot (9 by 29-meter) lot, with 3-foot (1 meter) sideyards and a small 15-foot-deep (4.5 meter) garden on the canal frontage.

The primary objective was to create a feeling of openness, despite the cramped site, and to connect all the primary spaces with the gardens and canal without sacrificing privacy. The public areas of the house front strongly on the canals with expansive sliding glass walls. An intimate garden courtyard on the eastside acts as a lightwell and provides a private garden view to the media room and bedrooms placed towards the middle of the site.

The rear of the house accommodates the reading and music room. A roof garden captures the treeline and sunsets of the beachside community and offers respite from the cramped siting of the canals. Much like a boat, movement through relatively compact and somewhat labyrinthine circulation is softened with radial and angled transitions.

Burton House

Kentish Town, London, UK
Ahrends Burton and Koralek

House area: 1,797 square feet/167 square meters
Studio/guest house area: 936 square feet/87 square meters
Site area: 3,175 square feet/295 square meters
Materials: Timber for structure, brick for walls and floors, glass and anodized aluminum for cladding and windows

This is a courtyard house formed by four structural pavilions with a linking conservatory. The house is entered through a round gate in the boundary wall, which flanks its eastern side. A glazed roof extends from end to end of the house, and forms a generous porch to the front door that opens into the conservatory leading to the house and court garden. The outlook is onto the gardens and the richly articulated backs of the houses to the south.

The house itself consists of three pavilions each with a similar structure in exposed timber, one pavilion extending to a first floor to house the master bedroom and bathroom. On the ground floor, the three linked spaces of dining/kitchen, sitting room, and study/guest room each have quite different atmospheres created by the varying ceiling design and use of glazing in walls and roof. The studio is a double-height pavilion.

The design takes a middle path view of energy conservation with comfort and delight playing their important parts in this aspect. Natural light, passive solar gain, and very good insulation are combined to contribute to the solution.

Caner/Beier Residence

Napa County, California, USA
Arkin Tilt Architects

Client: John Caner and George Beier
House area: 2,680 square feet/249 square meters
Site area: 20 acres/8 hectares
Materials: Wood frame with plywood and batten siding, corrugated metal roofing, concrete slab floors, stained, sprayed cellulose insulation, salvaged fir trusses, metal tie rod, purlins and salvaged cedar decking, insulated wood frame above, rammed earth at fireplace and loggia columns, site built pavers of stabilized earth

On a north–south axis, to fit into the hillside and opening up to the western view, the great room presented a passive solar challenge. The doors to the west are shaded by a deep loggia, the roof of which bounces light through the high windows to illuminate the ceiling. By holding down the roof of the kitchen, a high south-facing window allows light deep into the space. A dormer is added in the kitchen for both daylight and relief from the low ceiling.

The main spaces are of sprayed earth construction. Taking advantage of diurnal temperature fluctuations, the 18-inch thick (46-centimeter) earthen walls provide both thermal moderation as well as a rich, patinaed finish. Rammed earth is used at the fireplace and loggia columns for drama. A modern version of an ancient building system, the earthen walls give the structure a timeless quality. The thick walls are topped with a roof structure of recycled fir trusses and cypress decking salvaged from pickle barrels.

Stained concrete floors and the natural walls are balanced by a rich collection of salvaged materials, such as a recycled glass countertop and a piece of a bowling alley, chosen for their durability as well for their sustainability.

Canyon Residence

Los Angeles, California, USA
Steven Ehrlich Architects

House area: 7,400 square feet/687 square meters
Site area: 21,061 square feet/1,956 square meters
Materials: Wood framing, plywood, steel, cement plaster, copper, Douglas fir, Brazilian cherry wood, stone, stucco, glass

A series of vertical masses of colored burnished stucco form a structural-ordering element that aligns in the north–south direction. These masses house elements that serve the adjacent spaces such as fireplaces, stair, mechanical core, and storage. They cascade through the house responding to need while forming a kinetic rhythm of color and form. Counterpointing these vertical planes is a series of cascading copper-clad horizontal canopies. They protect natural wood, glass windows, and doors from rain and runoff and form a horizontal balance of floating planes that becomes part of the critical sculptural ordering system.

The ensemble of vertical colored mass in conjunction with the copper horizontal planes, glass, and painted stucco mass dances harmoniously as indoor space fuses into the natural environment.

The L-shaped parti embraces the grandeur of the sloping site adjacent to a creek. The house steps down following the site's slope and is never more than two stories at any location. An 18-foot-high (5.4 meter) living room area separates the two-story bedroom wing from the family-kitchen zone. The house strongly connects each indoor space to the verdant landscape beyond replete with native California trees around which the house has been designed. An amphitheater of stairs and floating decks facilitates this connection.

Cape Schanck House

Cape Schanck, Victoria, Australia
Denton Corker Marshall

The beach house on the coast south of Melbourne, Victoria, is located to enjoy expansive ocean views from the top of a very steep site in the middle of a golf course. The house looks northwest along the beaches of the Mornington Peninsula and southwest to Cape Schanck. It is pushed up above the dense cover of tea-tree with the single slot of a ribbon window peeping over the tree line.

The orthogonal black form is very clear and simple, but there is something odd to it. The box tube is twisted in section, the cladding raked, the lower windows cranked, the chimney emerging from the wall on the diagonal. The house looks nothing like a house, but rather like an object flying in from space and rotating along its long axis as it is about to land. The house is a dynamic enigma in the windswept setting.

Carmel House

Pebble Beach, California, USA
Cesar Pelli & Associates Inc

House area: 8,500 square feet/790 square meters
Site area: 2.5 acres/1 hectare
Materials: Stucco, Douglas fir, copper, mahogany, plaster

The house is organized around a central courtyard facing the bay and the southern sun. Three lines of circulation surround the courtyard and organize all of the functions of the house. The entry side, against the slope of the hill, is very low and has minimal openings to direct the occupant's view out to the landscape beyond. The main line of circulation starts at the main entrance, goes through a loggia, and terminates in an aerie with panoramic vistas to the mountains and the ocean, and is precisely sited to view the Bay as framed by two old and majestic Monterey pines. All primary functions including living room, kitchen, dining room, and master bedroom are located on the entry level to minimize the need for stairs by the residents.

The design of the house responds to the limitations and conditions of the site to take advantage of views or sun, and to meet site and code requirements, such as height limitations, a 5,000-square-foot (465-square-meter) site coverage, tree removal restrictions, and the need for drought- and deer-resistant planting. The cool and misty microclimate of the Monterey Peninsula led the architect to use year-round radiant floor heating systems, no air-conditioning and long lasting materials that will withstand the seasonal droughts and rains. The design also incorporates an intelligent house system with which the occupants can control lighting, window treatments, and an audio system.

Carter/Tucker House

Breamlea, Victoria, Australia
Sean Godsell

Client: Earl Carter and Wanda Tucker
House area: 2,269 square feet/210 square meters
Materials: Plasterboard, Victorian ash, stainless steel, Western red cedar

A three level 12 by 6-meter (39 by 19-foot) box was embedded into the side of a sand dune. The house has three rooms. The lower ground floor is for guests and the single space can be divided by a sliding wall into two rooms if required. Similarly the single space on the middle level can also be divided to separate the owners' bedroom from a small sitting area. The top floor is for living and eating and takes advantage of views across a rural landscape. The top floor is also a daylight photographic studio.

Carwill House

Stratton, Vermont, USA
Kohn Pedersen Fox Associates PC

Client: William and Carolyne Stutt
House area: 5,600 square feet/520 square meters
Site area: 5.7 acre/2.3 hectares
Materials: Vermont slate blocks, rough-hewn cedar planks, lead-coated copper roofing, fir cabinets and trim, cherry and marble floors, marble countertops, plastered gypsum-board walls and ceilings

The house is located within a residential development called High Meadow, in Stratton, Vermont. The specific site for the house is at the highest point within the development. It slopes very steeply to the south and faces directly towards Stratton Mountain. Hence, views to that mountain were a primary concern in the design solution. Large outcroppings were evident about the site.

The architect interpreted the clients' desire to link the intimate with the grand by interlocking a series of internal spaces. Throughout the composition there is a purposeful tension created by the juxtaposition of curvilinear and linear forms. The primary pieces—rotunda, main stair, and living room—stabilize the shifting forms.

The design solution was initiated by a severe slash cut through the rock, terminated by an outdoor fireplace. An entry court, facing Stratton Mountain, was formed by the rock face of this cut and the wall of the house. The key volumes are clad in lead-coated copper, as are the roofs, while the linear enclosing walls of the secondary spaces are clad in large planks of natural rough sawn cedar. The base of the house, as it meets the grade, is of Vermont slate.

Colorado House

Telluride, Colorado, USA
Architecture Research Office

House area: 10,000 square feet/929 square meters
Site area: 60 acres/24.2 hectares

This vacation home in a meadow on a mesa, has spectacular views of the untouched landscape and surrounding mountains. The clients required a house with spaces for large family gatherings, and intimate areas for personal contemplation of the wilderness. The house is conceived as a frame both for the landscape and for the client's museum-quality collection of 20th-century furniture and contemporary art.

Parallel walls step down a knoll, orienting the house towards specific views and establishing several interlocking interior spaces and levels. A computer model of a 15 x 17-mile (24 by 27 kilometer) section of the topography was made to check the view from each window. The house was oriented so that the Sneffels Range is seen between parallel walls, along their axis, and the Ophir Needles appear through openings in the walls. Each interior space opens to a different exterior space. Exterior walls of Corten shingles rest on sandblasted concrete foundations and at certain points the shingles slip into the house, accentuating the relationship between inside and outside.

Cozzens Residence

Washington DC, USA
McInturff Architects

When the client bought this prominently sited Georgetown house he thought it needed new bathrooms. Subsequent inspection revealed that the back of the house, having been built on 60 feet (18 meters) of fill, was migrating south.

New helical steel piers, some more than 60 feet (18 meters) long, have stabilized the movement of the structure and a new steel frame gives new rigidity to the four-story back addition that dated from the early 1970s. Removing a floor created a double-height volume from which to regard one of the best views in Washington. On the exterior, teak sunshades protect the new steel and glass façade from the southern sun. Inside, a wall of books extends up three stories. The bathrooms were also renovated.

Crescent House

Wiltshire, UK
Dr Ken Shuttleworth, Architect

Client: Dr Ken and Seana Shuttleworth
Materials: White finished concrete, glass

The house is modest and austere. Its simple form reacts strongly with the location, reflecting the various contrasts that the site offers as well as its historical context. The critical ingredients are a variety of spaces related to their function, a response to the changing quality of natural light, sensory contact with the elements of nature and the changing seasons, and a model for family living which is ecologically sensitive.

The concept is a series of simple, pure forms of white finished concrete and glass. Internally it creates different types of space related to the type of activity and varying quality of light. The normal clutter of architectural detail and designer items has been eliminated.

The design concept has two distinct, strongly contrasting sides. The northeast, which contains the private spaces, is adjacent to the other houses, the road, and poorer views, it presents a solid and translucent convex wall that increases privacy, reduces the effects of the westerly winds, and offers a robust, simple image to the approach. The southeast, with good views and exposure to the sun, is exactly the opposite—a concave crescent of clear glass reaches out to embrace the landscape and capture the views—offering maximum contact with nature from the living spaces. Between the two crescents is a double-height gallery and circulation

De Blas House

Madrid, Spain
Alberto Campo Baeza Arquitecto
in collaboration with Raúl Del Valle

Client: Francisco de Blas
House area: 2,368 square feet/220 square meters
Site area: 32,292 square feet/3,000 square meters
Materials: Concrete, steel, glass

This house has been placed at the crest of a north-facing hill with views to the mountains outside Madrid. It provides a settlement option for a plateau. A platform has been created from a concrete box, upon which a transparent glass box, with a delicate, white, light-steel roof placed on the concrete podium.

The poured-in-place concrete box at the base forms a cave that encases the traditional features of the house. The serviced rooms are to the front and the service spaces are to the rear.

One rises from within the house to the belvedere, which is a glass box placed on the platform. The cave below is a refuge. The space above is like an urn, and forms an area from which to contemplate the environment.

The entire project is confirmed by the precision of its dimensions. The concrete box is 9 by 27 meters (29 by 88 feet). The metallic structure is 6 by 16 meters (20 by 52 feet). The glass box is 4.5 by 9 meters by 2.3 meters high (15 by 29 feet by 7.5 feet).

The house attempts to be a literal translation of tectonic and stereotomic questions: a tectonic piece set upon a stereotomic box. It is a distillation of what is essential in architecture; once again, "more with less."

Defeo House Renovation

Venice, California, USA
OJMR Architects

House area: 1,450 square feet/135 square meters
Site area: 5,435 square feet/505 square meters
Materials: Concrete, wood frame, steel columns, plaster, Douglas fir, mahogany, white oak flooring, ceramic tile, maple cabinetry

This project incorporates a renovation of a 1938 one-story wood-frame house, with expansion to four bedrooms, three baths, kitchen, living area, adding an additional story and 1,200 square feet (111 square meters) of living space.

Through abstract diagramming, the walls have been expanded vertically and horizontally to open up the space to allow rooms to flow into one another. With four rectangular masses facing front, the roof was extended out over the front south-facing large glass windows and stretched back along a horizontal stream.

Slight angles, sloping rooflines, tilted-planes, and cutouts along the length of the house manipulate and carve the space to allow for maximum light to modulate throughout the house, as well as for natural cooling from ocean breezes to circulate. In deference to family life of the 1990s, the communal areas of living, eating, and cooking are free flowing. The architect eliminates the idea of separate living and family rooms in exchange for one large communal area. In addition, the private becomes public as a connection was forged between the community at large and the community within, through large street-facing glazing.

Dr Manke Residence

Melbeck, Germany
gmp – Architekten von Gerkan, Marg und Partner

Designers: Meinhard von Gerkan and Joachim Zais
Client: Susanne and Dr Michael Manke
House area: 3,767 square feet/350 square meters
Site area: 53,820 square feet/5,000 square meters
Materials: Reinforced concrete, masonry, red cedar, steel, tin, beech

The starting point for the design was the clients' own admiration of classical architecture using contemporary architectural elements. Two outbuildings and the main house create a courtyard facing the road that shield the living areas from the surrounding development. The outbuildings can accommodate four cars, storage for garden equipment, and cellar storage.

The house is entered through a hall which optically links the entrance level with the upper floor, whilst offering a view of the open landscape through the open sliding doors to the living area. The southern elevation of the house is fully glazed, with wooden sun shades and a projecting roof to filter the light and give protection from strong sunlight.

Drake House

Westchester, New York, USA
Alfredo De Vido Architects

House area: 6,000 square feet/557 square meters
Site area: 5 acres/2 hectares
Materials: Wood frame, concrete foundations, vertical cedar siding, sheetrock interior, wood ceiling in pool area

This rural land slopes gently towards a lake and is bounded by a cliff on one side and protected wetlands on the other. These factors limited the buildable area of the 5-acre (2-hectare) property. Two other important considerations in planning the house included the requirement for an indoor swimming pool and the desirability that as many rooms as possible face the view.

The architect's solution was to place the entry to the house at mid-level on the hill, with other rooms stepping up and down from it via internal stairs, and with rooms fitting into the hillside. In the central part of the house, space flows freely from area to area. Rooms are planned so that light comes into each from a variety of directions and windows reveal the view.

On the lowest level is the swimming pool area where a curved wall undulates towards the lake, adding a symbolic waveform to the water's edge. A Brazilian wood ceiling complements the blue of the water. Since higher rooms necessarily overlook lower portions of the house, spaces were designed to provide visual interest when seen from within. A palette of neutral stains accentuates the geometric variety.

Drysdale Residence

Atlantic Beach, Florida, USA
William Morgan Architects PA

House area: 1,630 square feet/151 square meters
Site area: 7,500 square feet/697 square meters
Materials: Cedar shingle siding, plywood, southern yellow pine, exposed wood floors and ceilings, painted gypsum wallboard

Elevated four floors above the surrounding coastal forest, the cantilevered decks and living spaces of the residence overlook the Atlantic Ocean several hundred feet to the east and the windblown forest to the west. Minimal openings in the walls to the north and south assure maximum privacy from nearby neighbors on the narrow suburban lot.

Bedrooms, baths, and dressing areas occupy the intermediate floors of the residence, while a generous carport and entry provides access from the ground level. Twin service towers brace the structure against the winds of occasional coastal storms and hurricanes. Stairs occupy the south tower; the north tower contains mechanical systems including plumbing and air-conditioning equipment.

Biaxial symmetry organizes the compact plan of the residence on each floor. Exposed roof rafters and floor joists placed in alternating centers impart a distinctive scale and rhythm to the interiors. Extensive overhangings and roofed porches protect the window walls from rain, glare, and solar heat.

Limited by a modest construction budget, material and labor-saving building methods were imperative. Construction economics included arranging the stair system to serve as a hallway, utilizing structural decking both as finished floors and as ceilings, and prefabricating the fourth floor and roof on grade for erection by a crane.

Gallery for Contemporary Art

Massachusetts, USA
Kennedy & Violich Architecture

Site area: 6 acres/2.4 hectares
Materials: Zinc cladding, cedar siding, glass mosaic tile

This project integrates a gallery addition into an existing residence with the design of an outdoor landscape for artworks on a wooded 6-acre (2.4-hectare) site. The hybrid program for this project includes a dance space, an office with high-tech telecommunication facilities, a pool, and gallery spaces for a collection of contemporary and modern art with two exterior courtyards and a sculpture garden. The design needed to accommodate this unusual program in a single, flowing space, provide maximum wall space for large-scale artworks, as well as smaller paintings and prints, bring views and natural daylight into the gallery spaces, and protect artworks from damaging UV light.

The design creates six contiguous, uninterrupted ceiling and roof planes to unite the existing residence with a series of new spaces that flow across a 48-foot-long (15 meter) pool of water. A habitable internal skylight well is suspended above the pool to reflect filtered western sunlight from the surface of the water into the galleries. At night, the light well functions as a quiet void space that bounces light off the ceiling to illuminate the gallery with ambient light.

The project redefines the hierarchies of domesticity, leisure, and the workplace, and proposes a new contemporary landscape for art that offers an alternative to the institutionalized spaces of art museums and galleries. The project provides new kinds of experiences between different functions that enable the clients to enjoy the artworks in intimate connection with activities of living and working.

Garden House

Atherton, California, USA
Olson Sundberg Kundig Allen Architects

House area: 10,441 square feet/970 square meters
Site area: 59,202 square feet/5,500 square meters

This house grew from the clients' travels to Japan and their desire to build anew where they had lived for the past 30 years. Deeply impressed by Kyoto's Katsura Palace, they wished to capture its spirit and translate it to our time and culture.

The integration of land, house, and art, and connections to the hilly landscape are paramount. There are three principal conceptual components: "the garden" (dining room, entry, and a gallery that can open to the garden); "the nest" (family room, kitchen, and bedrooms); and "the temple" (a pavilion for living and indoor art).

The garden is dominated by an allée of paired columns weaving together outside and inside space. Environmental art is installed there. The nest is more traditional, its two-story volume engages the hillside, reinforcing ideas of protection. The temple suspends reality and directs one's attention to spiritual or immaterial things. Subtly reflective soffit panels and a curved floating ceiling dissolve space and, in effect, expand time. Dominating the temple is a giant steel horse by artist Deborah Butterfield.

The Japanese influence can be felt not just in concept but in the details: the paired round wood-columns and their black metal shoes and caps; the skilled joinery of the wood beams above; and the entry door of planks bound together by large metal straps and hinges.

Three decades of family history motivated the decision to reuse the site, rather than build elsewhere. The garden was left as undisturbed as possible, and the idea of recycling carried over to wood-columns and flooring salvaged from old factories. Woods were left in their natural unpainted states. Colors, when used, are serene, tending toward gray, tan, and green. The result is a residence sympathetic to nature and the surroundings, providing an inspiring yet peaceful refuge for living.

Gibbs House

Eastbourne, Wellington, New Zealand
Parsonson Architects

Client: George and Keena Gibbs
House area: 2,863 square feet/266 square meters
Site area: 29.6 acres/12 hectares
Materials: Treated pine, corrugated colorsteel, painted fiber-cement sheet, plantation Eucalyptus Salingna

The client has a love for the New Zealand bush and a strong affinity with the site, which has been in the same family for four generations. Their desire was for a house with a natural spirit, connected to its setting, something that would provide a home for them in their impending retirement years and where they could welcome family and friends.

Entering the house, there is a sense of unfolding. From below, it is a solid, linear wall that hides the Beech Forest behind. Entry through this wall and upwards allows the forest and harbor to be viewed and the house to lighten and open up in different directions.

Abstract references are made to the forest with metaphor, lines, layers, light, and shadow. The roof of the main level has been separated from the walls on all four sides to extend the sense of lightness and delicacy of connection. This main level becomes a viewing platform for the different horizons with a layering of both openness and division between spaces. The majority of the views are through either the slender Beech trunks or fine members of the building.

Green Street Residence

Melbourne, Victoria, Australia
Six Degrees Architects

House area: 1,561 square feet/145 square meters
Site area: 1,367 square feet/127 square meters
Materials: Existing brick shell, glass, aluminum, timber, pebble mix, steel

When the current owners, an artist and a graphic designer, purchased this residence, it was suffering from a history of many renovations carried out by various owners, with differing degrees of building expertise. Originally a two-story Victorian terrace house, it had a 1960's aluminum shopfront window, concrete poured on top of a rotten timber ground floor, and a rabbit warren of timber and brick walls.

The house evolved in three stages over a number of years and on a tight budget. Rubbish was removed from the building, after the demolition of nearly all the internal building fabric, leaving only the original solid brick shell. In complete contrast to the numerous cramped spaces and corridors, four large spaces remained. A simple bench was also built to provide a working area for the kitchen and enable the owners to live in what was otherwise four large uncluttered spaces.

Rather than renovate the façade a new face was added, suspended over and preserving the 1960's aluminum shopfront and the remains of the original Victorian façade. A recomposed section of glass curtain wall retrieved from a General Motors factory in outer Melbourne, was bracketed to the existing façade, refacing the building and mediating the impact of the hot west sun.

The final brief was to provide upstairs with a bathroom, storage, two bedrooms, and a living space. A skylight was used to run the length of upstairs and links all the rooms. Rectangular forms were used to separate the uses. No physical connections to walls allow these objects to float, with glass being used to provide acoustic separation where absolutely necessary. Sliding screens separate a child's bedroom and safely screen a staircase. The upstairs living room functions with the insertion of horizontal planes on which to sit, store, or recline.

Greenwood House

Galiano Island, British Columbia, Canada
Helliwell + Smith • Blue Sky Architecture

House area: 3,000 square feet/279 square meters
Materials: Red cedar, copper, glass, sandstone, cherry flooring and cabinetry, tatami mats, gypsum board

Set on a shallow strip of land on the northwest edge of Galiano Island, one of the southern Gulf Islands of British Columbia, the house is bounded to the southwest by the water of Trincomali Channel and on the northeast by dense forest. The available site is constrained by setback requirements from both the high-tide line and the main island road that passes by above.

Paralleling the shoreline, a single 14-inch (35.5-centimeter) diameter ridge beam acts as the datum for a continuously modulated structural skeleton of 9-inch (22.8-centimeter) diameter rafters. Exposed at each end in a set of exterior rooms, this structural system reaches out into the landscape, suggesting the bleached bones of a large fish washed up on shore. The movements of the roof on the seaside are calibrated to water views, reflected light, existing vegetation, and the provision of shade. On the forest side, a continuous skylight provides cool, dappled forest light.

The roof framing connects with the ground through an ordered series of interior columns running the length of the building. Partitions between columns organize the program to generate small spaces. Programmatic divisions are further reinforced through the treatment of floor surfaces. Living areas and bedrooms are floored in wide cherry plank while the entranceway, kitchen, and utility areas are tied together by a continuous band of flagstones flooring.

Hamilton House

Vaucluse, New South Wales, Australia
Harry Seidler & Associates

Set on a large hilltop in Sydney's premier suburb, the site commands spectacular views of the city skyline to the west and the opposite shoreline to the north. The owners had always lived on the site and their previous old house was demolished, maintaining a magnificent old Angophora tree in the center of the entrance drive courtyard. The house is positioned behind the tree at the top of the site.

Solidity, the use of permanent materials, and luxuriously proportioned spaces set the keynote for the design of this three-story house. The essentially rectangular plan is surrounded by sumptuously curved forms, which respond to needs: balconies widen for outdoor furniture groups, the study "scoops in" more city views, and the focal spiral stair is lit from a circular roof dome. Over the entrance the roof projects in an S-shape horizontally and down vertically to give protection—its form mirrored in the two-story-high space inside, above the front doors.

Hammond Residence

Sunshine Coast, Queensland, Australia
Clare Design

Client: Charles and Cheryl Hammond
House area: 861 square feet/80 square meters
Site area: 42 acres/17 hectares
Materials: Corrugated Zincalume, durability class 1 hardwood, hoop pine plywood

In contrast to the vast surrounding landscape this dwelling is reduced to simple elements and is modest in scale, form, and budget. The remote site overlooks the panorama of the Sunshine Coast and the Pacific Ocean from south to north. The house is placed to take maximum advantage of aspect whilst carefully acknowledging both the climatic conditions and the rural setting. The site is within the Queensland cyclone region and the building is designed for a wind speed of 60 meters/second.

Due to its remote location, the house was planned to utilize many prefabricated and pre-cut components. The remoteness also forced the house to be self-sufficient which suited the client's wishes to minimize energy consumption and to employ basic ecological design principles. The reduction of energy and resource consumption together with the use of largely plantation timbers demonstrates that sustainable design strategies can by employed to substantial effect in small projects.

Whilst the house draws on the construction of traditional Queensland houses, it represents a synergy of building process and design which has a relevance and wider application in its low cost, planning, and structural simplicity. The construction of this house is a further development and adaptation of the "system" previously used in the Clare Residence and demonstrates the flexibility embodied in the approach.

Harbor Town Residence

Memphis, Tennessee, USA
Looney Ricks Kiss

House area: 3,500 square feet/325 square meters
Site area: 8,712 square feet/809 square meters
Materials: Stucco, travertine, carpet, veneered plywood, granite

This residence is located in the heart of a traditional neighborhood development. The architects were challenged by the owners' desires for functionality and aesthetics in a contemporary environment while also meeting the requirements of the development's design guidelines. The guidelines require that the fundamental elements found in classic, traditional residential architecture be maintained (for example a raised first-floor level, a front porch or entranceway, overall vertical proportions, and front-loaded garages as a secondary element).

The owners' program was to create a home that presented a strong, abstract, yet respectful image to the street; to maximize an appropriate scale and volume for interior spaces; and to accommodate the sometimes conflicting desires of a formal versus spartan interior.

An entry portal serves as the front porch and also provides a degree of separation between public and private spaces. The floor level of the entry portal and foyer is raised to comply with the development's design guidelines. The subsequent spaces of the home step down toward the rear terrace, helping to define and heighten the interior scale and volume.

House 2 for Two Architects

San Miguel de Allende, Mexico
House + House Architects

House Area: 2,000 square feet/186 square meters
Materials: Reinforced concrete, masonry, stucco, slate, river rock, tile, steel, concrete, wood

Filled with gardens and light, this home faces west on a quiet street four blocks from the historic center of the beautiful 450-year-old colonial town of San Miguel de Allende, Mexico. Entry, living, dining, and kitchen open onto a plant-filled patio. An arc of burgundy columns against a deep blue wall opens the master bedroom onto a private garden. The master bath embraces an ancient pomegranate tree, its tile mural in cobalt, ochre, green, and burgundy sparkling with droplets of filtered sunlight. Upstairs, each bedroom has a private balcony and share a covered terrace and bath; a cylindrical shower of polished green concrete topped with glass has an eternal view to the sky.

Sinuous stairs snake and frosted stars sparkle against the 20-foot-tall (6 meter) blue patio wall. Rusted steel sconces march in rhythm with skylights and railings. Grids of steel windows span floor to ceiling, linking inside to outside in an invisible embrace. Luscious colors of mango, cobalt, and soft green are limewashes toned with natural minerals. Red and ochre river rocks twist against a charcoal background in the courtyard. Shafts of light spill between square columns onto a 200-year-old carpenter's table, framed to become the 11-foot (3.3-meter) dining table. The home is modern, yet saturated with the deepest of Mexican tradition.

House at Toro Canyon

Montecito, California, USA
Barton Myers Associates Inc

Client: Vicki and Barton Myers
House area: 5,995 square feet/557 square meters
Materials: Structural steel, metal, concrete, stucco, plaster, aluminum, galvanized steel shutters

The house is comprised of a procession of four steel loft buildings positioned on three terraces that ascend the length of the site. The sequence of these structures utilizes the site contours to minimize the impact upon the landscape, while its north–south orientation takes maximum advantage of the southern exposure and beautiful views.

A re-circulating pool system is incorporated into the rooftops, transforming the structures into a series of terraced reflecting ponds. Spilling from one pool to another, the water cascades down the procession of rooftops. The pools serve as a fire-resistant roof assembly and insulation, and the pool atop the guesthouse is used as a lap pool.

Each building has an exposed structural steel frame, with metal deck framing and concrete retaining walls and floors. The structures are open, loft spaces enclosed by glazed aluminum sectional doors, which can be opened and closed to varying degrees. North-facing clerestory windows provide panoramic views to the mountain and provide ample natural ventilation by taking advantage of the ocean breezes that rise up the hillside. Galvanized rolling fire shutters above every opening protect from brush fires indigenous to the area and create a secondary envelope that provides additional insulation and sun control.

House for Sonoran Desert

Scottsdale, Arizona, USA
Swaback Partners

Client: Ron and Kay McDougall
House area: 9,074 square feet/843 square meters
Site area: 56,580 square feet/5,256 square meters
Materials: Native stone, copper, bronze doors, stucco infill, granite features, plaster walls and ceilings, stone floors, custom millwork

The topography of the site formed a natural bowl shape, all focused on a surrounding golf course and a horizon profile of dramatic mountains. Within the planned building footprint, the site rose 12 feet (3.6 meters) from the street to the far end. The site posed two main challenges; how to address the 12-foot-fall (3.6 meter) in the land, with all the best views being at the upper level; and how to place what would be nearly 12,000 square feet of enclosed area plus pools, terraces, and driveway without losing the beauty of the site.

The sloping site was addressed by overlapping two single level plans, each with its own garage. A curved floor plan focused all interior spaces on the most idealized views of the golf course and mountains beyond. Five exterior terraces were stepped to provide for a gracious transition between the upper and lower levels, with the pool occurring midway.

The principal exterior materials are dry-stacked native stone walls with copper roofs and fascias. Exterior doors are bronze clad and feature a design character that appears throughout the house. Interior features include custom furnishings, integrated sculpture, plant stands, and custom lighting.

House for the Future

Museum of Welsh Life, St Fagans, Cardiff, Wales, UK
Jestico + Whiles (Heinz Richardson, Jude Harris, Andy Piles)

Client: National Museums & Galleries of Wales
House area: 1,722 square feet/160 square meters
Site area: 7,535 square feet/700 square meters
Materials: Timber frame, wool insulation, cellulose fiber insulation, clayboard and clay plaster, oak rainscreen cladding, lime render

The National Museums and Galleries of Wales and BBC Wales commissioned a new house to stand alongside a collection of historic buildings, which comprise the Museum of Welsh Life at St Fagans, near Cardiff in Wales. The structure consists of a post-and-beam timber frame prefabricated with locally grown oak. A super-insulated wall of timber studwork wraps around three sides of the building, allowing maximum flexibility for window and door openings. This is faced externally with lime render and Welsh oak boarding. Sheep's wool in the walls and recycled newspapers in the roof provide high levels of insulation.

The house relies on a strategy of sensible energy use, assisted by passive technologies that are supported by easy-to-use control systems. It has been designed to make no net contribution to carbon dioxide emissions. It is highly insulated and features a ground source heat pump and a wood pellet heater, as well as passive solar gain supply heating. An active solar (water heating) and photovoltaic unit mounted at ridge level contribute to the power and hot water demands.

Planning of the internal living space is kept deliberately fluid to respond to the particular needs of the residents. Open living and daytime spaces are located to the south, whilst more private and enclosed cellular spaces are located to the north. The modular approach to the design allows the possibility for a number of variations to the base model according to spatial needs, a desire for flexibility, and available finance. A simple shell structure can be increasingly colonized as the circumstances of the residents alter with time and economics.

House in Aggstall

Bavaria, Germany
Hild und K Architekten BDA

Client: Barbara Gross and Bertold Schwartz
House area: 3,229 square feet/300 square meters
Site area: 21,538 square feet/2,000 square meters
Materials: Full brick, lightweight wooden brick, plaster, oak

The building is situated in a little hamlet close to Freising in Upper Bavaria. Standing on a north slope, it points southwards and towards a large garden. Instead of a rundown estate consisting of various extensions, it was decided to develop a detached family house with approximately 300 square meters (3,229 square feet) of living space. One of the essential requirements of the licensing authorities was to maintain the original ridge height as well as the length and width of the old property.

The exterior façade is a reflection of the irregularity and shadow play of the traditional, plastered stone structure. The façade was cast with a corn yellow rough plaster with the color repeated on the roof and pedestal. The interior rooms are decorated with simple plaster, with windows and floors made of oak.

House in Mt Fuji

Fujiyama, Yamanashi Prefecture, Japan
Satoshi Okada architects

Client: Sei Torii and Shunsuke Tomiyama
House area: 1,410 square feet/131 square meters
Site area: 8,557 square feet/795 square meters
Materials: Oak flooring, granite, Japanese cedar, plaster board, Japanese cedar, granite, asphalt-sheet roofing, aluminum sash

The house stands on the northern foothills of Mt. Fuji, on an ancient lava bed. Appearing as a shadow in the forest, an upheaval among silvery birch, beech, and magnolia, the building settles into a shallow depression on the site, bounded on two sides by roads.

The building is a wood-framed structure, clad externally with Japanese cedar plates stained in black. The larger section is a double-height living room with a skylight, extending onto a terrace. Stairs lead to a gallery running along the front of the building, underneath part of which is a kitchen/dining area. In the private part on the triangular hall, there are two bedrooms, one stacked above the other. At the back, the building steps down to provide bath and shower rooms and a covered balcony for the lower bedroom.

The back wall of the living room sheers off towards the opposite wall of the house so that space is suddenly compressed into a narrow corridor that leads to the entrance and double-height hall. Adjacent, the dining/kitchen area is compressed to a 2 meter ceiling height, which provides a feeling of comfort. Such devices create the illusion of greater space, the impression of movement, and the variety of scenes of architectural space.

House in the Connecticut Hills

Connecticut, USA
Mark Simon, FAIA & James C. Childress, FAIA, Centerbrook Architects and Planners

House area: 1,350 square feet/125 square meters
Site area: 15 acres/6 hectares
Materials: Vertical cedar siding, lead-coated copper standing seam roof, wide-board pine flooring

This little house serves as the main house and entry gate to an estate of large trees, rolling lawns, and carefully gardened rock outcroppings. Approached from downhill it is at first apparently symmetrical. On closer inspection, its five parts—dining/living room wing, bedroom/study wing, central vestibule, and two chimneys—declare their gentle independence from one another.

The two pavilions are set at slightly different angles to the center, and the chimneys are of different sizes and angles. The living/dining pavilion is a large space with a cathedral ceiling, with a fireplace at one end and a kitchen at the other. Three French doors march down each side for light in the winter and breezes in the summer. At the end above the kitchen is a large Venetian window with its side panels dropped to the floor. Overhead cross-ties have been doubled to hide lamps illuminating silk draperies on alternate bays. These and the French doors give a gentle ambient illumination, important to one of the clients whose eyes are sensitive to bright light.

A similar lighting treatment is used in the other pavilion above the master bed where drapes are also hung from bay to bay. Tucked next to the bedroom are two bathrooms and a small study with floor-to-ceiling books, a fireplace of its own, and additional indirect lighting.

House in the Hudson Valley

New York, USA
Jefferson B. Riley, FAIA & Charles G. Mueller, AIA, Centerbrook Architects and Planners

House area: 5,500 square feet/511 square meters (addition); 2,760 square feet/256 square meters (existing)
Site area: 100 acres/40.4 hectares
Materials: Red cedar clapboards and tongue and groove vertical boards, red cedar shingle roofing, maple stairs and floors, natural vertical grain fir in Great Room

This large addition extends outward from a 19th-century farmhouse that now appears from its country road as a string of traditional, connected barns. To passersby on the road, the "barns" conceal the large size and complexity of the dwelling. It contains a gymnasium and exercise room, spa, great room, bunk room, office, summer room, gardens, terraces, and a pool house serving an existing pool. The complex was designed to transport the owners out of their work-a-day world to one of maximum physical and emotional comfort.

An informal entry gate leads into an intimate and fragrant herb garden where views of the whole complex unfold. Stone walls create outdoor terraces and places to sit overlooking the pool and a small lake beyond. Inside, fir paneling and stylized "trees" used in the great room recall the owners' love affair with Adirondack lodges and the forests that surround their property. The bunkroom perches in the upper reaches of the great room, as might a tree house.

Triple-hung windows convert the summer room into a screen porch on pleasant days. The gymnasium contains a half court for basketball and a windowed exercise room overlooking the vegetable garden, while the spa's jacuzzi tub has a private view of the miniature Zen rock garden. The office, which has its own outdoor entrance, commands panoramic views of the property. The kitchen in the original house was renovated with Shaker-style cabinets and granite countertops shaped and colored in the images of breakfast fruit.

House in the Rocky Mountains

Genesee, Colorado, USA
Alexander Gorlin Architect

This house is organized along two axes, forming a pinwheel plan inserted into the site between two ravines. Stone walls that form the image of a ruin "found" in the inhabited wilds are re-inhabited with the program of the house. These vertical surfaces echo the nature of the site, while mediating between the exterior and interior spaces of the house.

From the drive, which opens into an exterior court, the visitor enters the house by bridge over a ravine, penetrating a massive stone wall. Along this wall, a compressed terrace corridor allows access to the primary public spaces of the house. The wall terminates into the mountainside from which a tower is projected. On the roof of the tower, an exterior room provides a view to the stepped roof terraces of the house.

House Into
Espoo, Finland
Jyrki Tasa

Client: Into Tasa
House area: 2,013 square feet/187 square meters
Site area: 24,111 square feet/2,240 square meters
Materials: Steel, wood, plywood, glass brick, soapstone, concrete, cherry wood

Standing lightly on the rock and protected by the curving wall, the house extends towards the evening sun. The building is organized into clear-cut sectors and its appearance is contemporary in form as well as in material, conveying rationality and diversity.

The road leads the visitor towards the white protective wall. The undulating eaves and tall, oblique steel columns of the west front are only partially visible, giving a hint of the binary character of the house. The visitor crosses a steel bridge above a pool and arrives at a tall glass cut made in the white wall—the main entrance. The neighboring buildings are left behind on crossing the bridge and what is left is the natural surroundings, readily open both within and without the house, on its balconies and terraces.

After the entrance there opens a view through the high glazed wall to the large terrace and the sea. The high-ceilinged entrance hall is the heart of the house, integrating the various spaces both functionally and visually. The bedrooms and the sauna are on the left side of the entrance floor and the swimming pool is on the right. On the first floor the kitchen is on the left, with the adjacent dining area and morning coffee balcony, while on the right side there is the living room with its afternoon sun balcony. The entrance area has a visual connection to the basement, where there are hobby and utility spaces, and a door to the parking area beneath the terrace.

House rue Robert Blache
Paris, France
Architecture Studio

House area: 1,410 square feet/131 square meters

Located in Paris, rue Robert Blache is part of a heterogeneous quarter between the Gare de l'Est and the Saint Martin Canal. The project builds a four-story town house over an existing ground floor thus filling up the empty space between two existing buildings.

It aims to push the restrictions of the envelope allowed by the zoning regulations to the limit, to recover the orthogonal setting with the street and to bring the sun to the furthest corners of the house. Two white concrete volumes are attached to existing buildings and take on the rounded roof shape typical of 19th-century Paris.

At the center of the house is a steel staircase contained in a deployed metal cage, which looks like an aviary. It divides the premises into rooms overlooking the street and others overlooking the courtyard, offset by half a level from the others.

Island Vacation House
Bay of Islands, New Zealand
Pete Bossley Architects

Materials: Fijian Kauri plywood, cedar walls, oak flooring and cabinetry

The house has been carefully sited on an idyllic island, set amongst its rich canopy. The timber house, which exhibits a lightness and transparency, is as memorable as the breathtaking views.

The external walls are full-height framed joinery units, and the internal walls are cedar boards to door-height, with glazing to the roof. As a result, the timber-lined roof appears to float above the house. The view across the water becomes one continued panorama and an ever-changing backdrop. The sun, natural ventilation, and outdoor spaces are carefully controlled by the roof, which gradually widens to provide a more protective canopy over the living area terraces.

As one moves down the levels towards the living areas; the house appears to open up and become more transparent. While the home is only one-room wide on each level, the series of outdoor decks ensure that the location can be enjoyed from every room of the house and at any time of the day.

While the house appears the epitome of simplicity, it has been meticulously designed. The kitchen, dining, and living areas not only demonstrate a change in floor level, but a subtle change in proportion, with the living area opening generously to the wonderful northern light. The house represents some of the most precious aspects of beach living, a wonderful shelter that is also close to its environment.

Jackson House
Bermagui, New South Wales, Australia
Daryl Jackson Architects

Client: Daryl and Kay Jackson
House area: 3,983 square feet/370 square meters
Materials: Timber, corrugated iron, cement render to concrete brickwork, timber-framed windows

The house is a collection of rooms held together by a high wall, which folds around the contoured hilltop to create the interior—an open courtyard edged by a large veranda. The rooms are connected only by the exterior, providing a cellular monastic separation. The elevation is a consistently structured section, the skillion reflecting the land contours.

J Residence
Seodaeshin-dong, Pusan, Korea
Kim Young-Sub + Kunchook-Moonhwa Architects

Client: Jung Yeon-Tae
House area: 5,037 square feet/468 square meters
Site area: 10,807 square feet/1,004 square meters
Materials: Paint on cement mortar, paint on brick

The main design elements of the house are the frame, wall, and box, which display a constructive layout. However, the bridge and stairway that connect or pass through each element, the overlapping walls, annexed pillars, and beams display a deconstructive image as they are afforded a degree of freedom pursuant to their subordinate functions. Nevertheless, when taken into consideration as a whole, these elements serve the function of refining and increasing the constructive architectural features, while also performing their given physical functions very well without any exaggeration.

The building was constructed in an L-shape along the boundary line of the site that is adjacent to a road, in order to take into consideration the directional exposure of the house and to segregate the inside space and the garden from the road. The eastern side of the house is a closed façade, which serves the dual purpose of blocking the inside view as well as piquing the curiosity of those passing by. The layout of each room in the living area is focused on the direction of and view from each room, while the gallery lies between the south and west. Although there is nothing new about the long corridor, it would be recognized as a deliberate attempt in a composite building of this size. Entry into and exit from the gallery below the connecting corridor is much lower than the garden level, so that entry from the road is easy.

Jamie Residence
Escher GuneWardena Architecture
Location: Pasadena, USA

House area: 2000 square feet/185.8 square meters
Site area:
Materials:

This project, designed as a family house for a young couple with a child, is located on a steeply sloping hillside at the north end of a canyon in the city of Pasadena (adjacent to Los Angeles). It looks over a golf course, the Rose Bowl Stadium and the city beyond, and there are also views of the San Gabriel Mountains to the east and the San Rafael Hills to the west.

The clients required a 2,000-square-foot house with three bedrooms, a study, a family/play room, and an outdoor deck, in addition to more formal living and dining areas. Most importantly, they wished to maintain access to as much of the dramatic vista as possible.

A design concept evolved from the most elegant structural solution on hand, which was to build two large concrete piers that carry two steel beams spanning an 84-foot length, which also carry the wood-framed house. These two piers are the only elements to meet the ground, causing minimal impact to the existing slope and allowing the natural landscaping to continue beneath the house. Access to the house is by a bridge that connects to the road on the uphill side of the property.

Views from all rooms at the perimeter are maintained, with the garage placed in the middle. The house is divided into two zones: one comprises an area for formal entertaining, the parents' bedroom suite and study; and another zone consists of the kitchen/breakfast area, the family/play room, and the children's rooms. The house is further divided into more enclosed spaces for bedrooms (facing the hillside), and very open spaces for communal activities (facing the view). These open spaces, which include the living, dining, outdoor deck, kitchen, and family rooms are all interconnected, to create one continuous 84-foot-long space with 180-degree views of the cityscape below and landscape beyond.

The exterior elevations of the house are composed of floor-to-ceiling window openings alternating with solid planes clad in a cement board panel system.

Kebbell House

Te Horo, Kapiti Coast, New Zealand
John Daish Architects + The Walls Organisation (T.W.O.)

Design direction: Sam Kebbell
Project Team: John Daish, Rafe Maclean, Daniel Watt
Client: Adrienne and Arthur Kebbell
House area: 1,453 square feet/135 square meters
Site area: 5.7 acres/2.3 hectares

The site is amongst several orchards, native trees, and some sheep paddocks one hour north of central Wellington. Our clients required a small one-bedroom house that was compact, light, and encouraged a relaxed lifestyle. The design addresses the warm climate and the powerfully raw landscape in several ways—the ground floor opens to the north and northwest, views of the plains are available to the upstairs bedroom, and the bathroom looks over a group of existing native trees. The kitchen runs into the landscape via the lap pool in one direction and aligns with rows of apricot trees in the other. The carefully detailed interior opens into a landscape of timber batten fences, trees, and long grass.

Kline Residence

Malibu, California, USA
Lorcan O'Herlihy Architects

House area: 5,800 square feet/539 square meters
Site area: 9,150 square feet/850 square meters
Materials: Steel moment frame and wood platform framing on concrete foundation, cement stucco, channel glass, aluminum, painted steel, painted aluminum sheet metal, skim coat plaster, birch plywood, Douglas fir doors

The house sits on a steeply sloping lot which faces the Pacific Ocean. The client requested roof terraces and maximized views to the ocean. As such, the house was conceived as both a shelter and an outlook. The deep vertical section of the site and its relation to wonderful views suggested the stereometric staggering of volumes along the steep slope of the site. Given the slope and its relation to views and structure, volume and light were used as the root to the architectural solution.

The silhouette of the house echoes the slope. Working with proportion and light, the living spaces are broken into a series of volumes supported by a structural steel frame. In section, the house is a layering of trays from the lowermost garage through the reception zones to the master suite above; a freestanding elliptical pavilion is sited at the high end of the lot, and is intended as an independent unit for guests. The steel frame lifts the ocean-side end high in the air to be enclosed by clear and translucent channel glass. Furthermore, it enables the breaking down of the constituent parts of the building: the interior life of the house is activated by extending itself to the exterior via the transparent walls.

Koivikko House

Helsinki, Finland
Architect Esa Piironen

House area: 1,571 square feet/146 square meters
Site area: 13,455 square feet/1,250 square meters
Materials: Concrete blocks, timber, steel

Town planning from the beginning of the 1960s permitted a confused, unplanned construction phase. Koivikko House is a mark of respect to the redevelopers. It is a late reply to the question of how an additional building can be planned to suit the environment, while taking into account factors that influence architecture, such as tradition, climate, environment, views, and mental images.

The interior of the house is a kind of revival of the post-war rebuilding scheme: a central chimney surrounded by rooms. The two-story living room, as a visual center space, adds life to the old scheme. The house is closed towards the street and opens itself through a greenhouse into the west-facing garden.

The design is based on the extra space requirements of a family of four, working on the assumption that it can later be used as a separate, self-contained unit. The house is also a tribute to handcrafts: the cellar is built from concrete blocks, and the aboveground floors of timber structures with exterior steel trimming.

Kronenberg Beach House

Killcare, New South Wales, Australia
Alexander Tzannes Associates

Materials: Steel, timber

The Kronenberg House at Killcare is designed for holiday use. The location is a steeply sloping coastal block of land. The interior planning provides flexible arrangements for changing use requirements including operable walls and a unique bed/desk/lounge transformation of in-built furniture. The exterior is clad in zinc with a marine-grade plywood soffit attached to the underside of the house. The interior is characterized by the use of timber, including blackbutt floor finishes, and hoop pine plywood walls and joinery, contrasting with warm white paint finishes. The rear deck is constructed from tallow wood and is finished with a natural gray stain.

Lawson-Westen House

West Los Angeles, California, USA
Eric Owen Moss Architects

Clients: Tracy Western and Linda Lawson

The Lawson-Westen House is an exploratory building, a perpetual investigation of the clients' wants and needs, and the use of the unconventional conventionally and the conventional unconventionally, to meet them. Linda Lawson and Tracy Westen, the clients, were essential to what this house came to be.

This three-story house is a hybrid of a cylindrical and a conical volume, each centered on a separate axis. The kitchen as the hub of family and social life, became the focal element of the building and is prominently located on the first floor. Simplistically, the kitchen is a double-height cylinder with a conical roof. The top of the cone is cut off creating an ocean view deck. The cone is also sliced vertically, resulting in a parabolic curve. The curve sets up an idealized vault, the edge of which the house never fully extends to with the exception of a single beam at the entrance.

The kitchen mapped in plan, sets up a pattern of points suggestive of an inner logic. But as the system is interpreted in the section, the connection between the hypothetical logic of the plan and the reality of the section is diminished. The sectional consequences do not give back to the plan.

Lewton Residence

Albuquerque, New Mexico, USA
Westwork Architects, PA

Client: George and Judy Lewton
House area: 3,423 square feet/318 square meters
Materials: Masonry, synthetic finish on stucco on wood frame, gypsum board on wood framing, stone and carpet floor finishes

The jagged forms of this house echo the geology of the nearby mountains. Rising up out of its site, the residence wraps around an east-facing courtyard to capture views of the mountains and provide an indoor/outdoor living and entertaining space.

A colonnade of steel columns leads through the courtyard space to the main entry. The living/dining/kitchen space at the heart of the house has a soaring ceiling and a clerestory window that catches the mountain crest profile. A vaulted pavilion-like form located at the east courtyard area houses the master bedroom and bath and offers a counterpoint to the hard-edged forms of the main house.

Malibu Beach House

Malibu, California, USA
David Lawrence Gray Architects

Materials: Concrete, steel, glass, teak, limestone

Located in the Malibu area, this beachside house overlooks the expansive Pacific Ocean. The design emerged from a philosophy about beachside living mixed with a desire for permanence in the face of harsh natural elements. A relaxing environment melds with lasting materials in order to withstand ocean winds, while being oriented around beautiful ocean views. Because the clients wanted the house to be low maintenance, materials like concrete and steel were selected. Board-formed concrete walls accentuate a richly textured interior filled with light and warmed by nautically inspired teak wood paneling. Surrounding views inspire a series of transparent glazing elements that give a sense of openness and expansiveness while shading devices and visual screens allow for privacy.

Conceptually the house was conceived as two distinct blocks linked with a cascading stair and waterfall that originates at the street and flows through the court and main house all the way to the surfside dunes. Art pieces by Frank Stella, Deborah Butterfield, Robert Graham, and George Rickey and a contemporary palette of glass, steel, teak, and limestone help to reinforce the relaxing yet durable nature of the project. The overall planning scheme results in a stark contrast between the turbulent setting of the ocean and the serene interior courtyard and pool.

Malibu Residence

Malibu, California, USA
Gwathmey Siegel & Associates Architects

House area: 14,700 square feet/1,366 square meters
Site area: 3 acres/1.2 hectares
Materials: Poured-in-place concrete, steel frame, wood-framed floors and walls, stucco exterior walls finish, standing seam zinc metal, limestone pavers, bluestone cobblestone, teak exterior, mahogany interior

This private residence is located on a 3-acre (1.2-hectare) site defined by the Pacific Coast Highway to the north, the Pacific Ocean to the south, and existing two-story residences to the east and west. The intention of the design was to create the perception of an expansive site, as well as to maximize the size of the building to accommodate an extensive program.

The tree-lined entry drive along the western edge of the site screens the guesthouse and tennis court to the east. The drive ends in a landscaped autocourt, which acts as a transition between the guest house/lawn area and the main house and pool area, located at the southern edge of the site, parallel to the bluff and ocean. To maximize views and introduce an architectural scale appropriate to the size of the site, the living/dining/kitchen and master bedroom are elevated to the second floor.

At ground level the entry separates the garage and service areas from the children's bedrooms, and allows direct access to the pool terrace. A circulation zone runs parallel to the two-story exterior glazed wall, connecting both full and half levels of the house physically and visually. A ramp leads from the entry to the first half level where it is terminated by the master bedroom. There, a spiral stair leads to a sleeping loft, oriented towards the ocean, and overlooking the sitting room below. The second floor provides a loft-like sequence of living/dining/kitchen spaces open to views of the ocean.

Mallet House

New York, New York, USA
SITE Environmental Design, Inc

House area: 3,300 square feet/306 square meters
Site area: 1,350 square feet/125 square meters

The residence was designed for the president of a fashion design company and her family in the Greenwich Village area of New York City. The project called for the renovation and expansion of an 1820's three-story, Greek Revival house in a historic landmark community. The dwelling was originally developed as early speculative housing. Because of neglect, economical construction methods to begin with, and general deterioration, the structure required major architectural work. Also, in order to expand the interior space, an innovative room was designed under the back garden and the basement converted to several bedrooms.

The concept for the interior of this house is based on a layering of narrative ideas, drawn from its history, its context, and from the personal biography of the owner. This information was converted into a series of architectural and furniture artifacts which partially emerge from the walls, like ghosted memories which have been invaded by later additions and by the presence of several generations of inhabitants. This choice of artifacts has been determined by the scale and purpose of each room, as well as by the already existing architecture.

Marquand Retreat

Washington, USA
The Miller/Hull Partnership, LLP

Client: Ed Marquand
House area: 450 square feet/42 square meters
Site area: 200 acres/81 hectares
Materials: Concrete block, wood decking, metal roofing, wood windows

The Naches River East of Yakima flows from the Cascade Mountains to the east and has carved out a beautiful valley rimmed by basalt cliffs. Attracted to the arid climate, the client purchased a 200-acre (81-hectare) "bowl" on the slope of a mountain. The site faces down into the river valley and cliffs beyond, and will be used for weekend getaways. The owner set the design challenge: to construct a limited, two-room program using materials that were resistant to fire, wind, and intruders. The client initially had notions of doing a project reminiscent of an Italian hill tower. However, the principle idea was to produce a design that was truly "western" in character without being nostalgic.

The structure was conceived as a thin metal roof floated across a basic concrete rectangle. The floating roof provides a shaded porch to the south, clerestory window slots at the main shell, and a covered path out to the water cistern tower to the rear of the building. A 10 by 10 foot (3 by 3 meter) opening faces south under the porch, with two full-size sliding doors hung on a track running the entire length of the wall. With one door screened and one glazed, the owner can customize the proportion of open ventilation to glazed area. The design had to respond to the potential for both blistering heat and freezing cold. However, the owner still wanted natural light and an architecture that expressed the raw quality of the site.

Without permanent power, the structure is effectively heated by a wood stove. The cistern is filled by a water truck, with plans for a well to be dug in the future.

Marsh House

Nottingham, UK
Marsh & Grochowski

House area: 1,830 square feet/170 square meters
Site area: 10,979 square feet/1,020 square meters
Materials: Brick, red quarry tile, sandstone, stained timber, stainless steel, Douglas fir, Perspex

The house consists of two main elements, one of three stories and one of two. The three-story element is sited to the north and cut into the hillside, so that from the street it appears only two stories high. The two-story element is sited to the south and east to give the three-story element clear views. The two are joined by means of a glazed circulation area. The three-story element straddles between two bookend-like towers, one of brick and one of stone.

The conceptual challenge was to make a house that was both private and intimate whilst at the same time responding to the beautiful surrounding, and allowing the garden and the seasonal nature of the British weather to become part of the interior. Particular responses to the context are expressed by the use of materials to carry out tasks for which they were not intended. Balustrades are formed from lengths of continuous bicycle chain stretched over gear cogs, obscure windows are made by inserting thousands of marbles between sheets of glass, and shop display systems are used to form library shelves.

In order to give an awareness of light and season, and to settle the house very specifically within its context, building elements are carefully placed to reinforce significant views from the site and semi-concealed roof lighting is introduced into the deeper parts of spaces to allow in the light. This is further developed with the use of Perspex floors and bridges within the interior.

Maxman House

Philadelphia, Pennsylvania, USA
Susan A. Maxman, FAIA

House area: 4,200 square feet/390 square meters
Site area: 21,780 square feet/2,023 square meters
Materials: Structural clay tile, stucco, cast stone, slate roof

The house was designed by George Howe, who along with William Lescaze is best known for the PSFS building, the United State's first international style skyscraper. Like the urban dwellings of Europe, the house shows its back to the street, and the chimneystack rises next to the front door.

The renovation maintained much of the original design. The house was opened up to light and a view of the garden by eliminating doors wherever possible, widening doorways, and converting small windows into French doors or picture windows in the kitchen. A narrow hallway was widened and sections of a wall removed to open up the living room to the rest of the first floor.

Making the house more livable not only required updating mechanical systems, remodeling the kitchen and introducing contemporary lighting, it also meant creating spaces that are comfortable to be alone in or with family and friends. Built-in bookcases surround the living room hearth and the kitchen was reconfigured with elements of warmth such as a bead board, a bookcase, and a window seat.

Mellangoose House

Falmouth, Cornwall, UK
Rod McAllister

Client: Lola and Bruce McAllister
House area: 1,884 square feet/175 square meters
Site area: 7,212 square feet/670 square meters
Materials: Load-bearing blockwork, pre-cast floors, cement render and softwood carpentry

The house was a low budget, self-build project using local masons and carpenters. The simply stacked bedrooms and aquamarine tiled bathrooms contrast with open, terraced living space. The arrangement occupies a cluster of terracotta volumes which spill down a mature orchard, either side of a narrow top-lit slot, towards a timber deck set within a sea of bamboo. The bright major spaces are double height for the display of the owner's large paintings. The kitchen work surfaces and the dining table were cast in concrete on site.

Michaels/Sisson Residence

Mercer Island, Washington, USA
The Miller/Hull Partnership LLP

Materials: Steel, concrete, metal, wood

Situated on a steeply sloping, wooded site alongside a small stream, this residence includes two main stories above a two-story concrete block base containing service spaces. An industrial palette of materials—steel, concrete, and metal—were chosen not only for their aesthetic appeal, but also for ease of maintenance.

An entry stair tower cantilevers off its foundation, protecting the roots of nearby Douglas fir trees. This stair leads visitors past the first floor that contains two purposefully cubby-like children's bedrooms; a bathroom; a small play area; laundry and mechanical storage.

As one continues up the stairs, the landing widens to provide space for a small computer area and library outside the path of circulation.

The upper two stories cantilever off the lower level garage and bedrooms in an effort to minimize the building footprint on the site. On the main level, the kitchen, living, and dining areas open onto a deck to an expansive view of the wooded ravine. The upper floor contains space for an electronic music room and is connected to the master bedroom via a bridge overlooking the living space below.

Moen Residence

West Des Moines, Iowa, USA
Herbert Lewis Kruse Blunck Architecture

Client: Michael and Christine Moen
House area: 7,900 square feet/734 square meters
Materials: Black stained ash, limestone, black granite, stainless steel, veneer plaster, sanded glass

The house was an ambitious reflection of an array of both passive and active solar concepts in a strong, modernist vocabulary of building elements. With south-facing overhangs, earth-covered roofs, tile floors, and an open floor plan, it responded to far-reaching concerns of energy conservation.

Over the next 25 years, nearly all the initial precepts of the house were challenged by the owners, resulting in extensive and pervasive modifications. The result was a house divided, devoid of any rational circulation system and decorated with plush carpets, patterned wallpapers, mirrored walls, and traditional furniture.

The project reconstructs, reconsiders, and reinterprets the original design. Begun by stripping nearly every surface back to the original structural concrete walls, concrete floors, and pre-cast roof decks, spaces were reordered along a circulation spine on both upper and lower levels. Interior living space was opened once again to expansive southern exposures. Carpets and ceramic tiles were replaced with either limestone or honed black granite.

A palette of black stained ash, limestone, black granite, stainless steel, veneer plaster, and sanded glass were used to define rooms and delineate building parts. The primary interest was to create restrained and ordering living spaces that provided a backdrop for a developing collection of furniture and art.

Muskoka Boathouse

Point William, Ontario, Canada
Shim Sutcliffe Architects

Like Le Corbusier's rustic cabin in southern France, or the Adirondack camps of upstate New York, this project is a "sophisticated hut" in the wilderness. The interlocking elements that align building and nature, land and water, and ultimately tradition and progress, define the experience of the boathouse. The vertical layers of the project form a threshold between the inner roof garden and the water's edge to complete the space defined naturally by the edge of the forest. As the ceiling planes are reflected in the water below, materials and methods are interwoven in the horizontal layers of the project to intensify the spatial expanse of the views oscillating between the woodland and the lake beyond.

The interweaving of the layers was created with a unique building sequence that began with the dock layout on the frozen lake. The position of each crib was drawn and a hole cut into the ice. As each crib was completed it was filled with granite ballast and lowered to settle on the lakebed. From this primitive submerged structure, the heavy timber outer walls emerge to protect an intricately crafted sleeping cabin. Interior finishes further intertwine the ordinary and the sophisticated. Cabinets of Douglas fir panels and intricate mahogany windows are detailed to allow differential settlement from movement in the crib foundations. Traditional Victorian beadboard ceilings are transformed into a shaped Douglas fir ceiling in the sleeping cabin. Mahogany duckboards in the bathroom echo the typical Muskokan wooden boat deck.

n-House

Kamakura, Kanagawa, Japan
Atelier Hitoshi Abe

The site is situated in the heart of a well-known historical city. This place may be described as a sanctuary, still blessed with an abundance of natural greenery. Located at the foot of a hill, it is surrounded by descending slopes on the north and west, and a precipitous bluff leading up to a hilltop on the south. Compared to ordinary housing sites, a considerable number of requirements define the organization of this place, including topographical conditions and legal restrictions, along with other regulations.

The client's requests included specially formulated black concrete, separate private rooms for the husband and the wife, apart from their Japanese-style main bedroom, two guest rooms, bathrooms adjacent to each room, and independent from the dining room, kitchen, and living room, a space for accommodating large gatherings.

Thus the characteristic shape of this house is a result of the internal requirements being replaced by a linked chain of alternate solids and voids. This chain forms a ring to create common spaces, and is then placed amongst the landscape of external requirements.

Nomentana Residence

Lovell, Maine, USA
Mack Scogin Merrill Elam Architects

Client: Margaret Nomentana
House area: 4,450 square feet/413 square meters
Site area: 2.8 acres/1.1 hectare
Materials: Wood and steel frame on concrete foundations, cementitious fiberboard and pre-weathered zinc cladding, concrete floors, wood and aluminum window and glazing systems

A modest site yields an intimate view across a pond to Lord's Hill, the eastern-most boundary of the White Mountains National Forest. The hill, an inclined plane approaching the vertical, comforts with summer-spring greenery, dazzles with fall colors, shimmers and glistens in winter snow and ice.

The house perches at the brink of the downward slope to the pond. Breathing in the site, the house transfigures it through a series of internal spatial events—framing, focusing, enclosing, extending, dismissing, and celebrating. Relocated from the farm to the forest, the house refers to and reinterprets the "big house, little house, back house, barn" of the famous children's rhyme.

Like Maine houses before it, the house is a result of form added on to form, spaces adjoining defensively and closely clustering, resisting long, harsh, Maine winters, and giving the impression of small "house-towns." Always looking back on itself, the rooms of the house are never alone. They are rooms always in visual and spatial communication. The house is rural and remote but not in isolation.

O Residence

Tokyo, Japan
Kisho Kurokawa Architect & Associates

House area: 3,315 square feet/308 square meters
Site area: 9,870 square feet/917 square meters
Materials: Red granite, concrete, wood, tatami mat, cedar, marble

The ground level of O Residence is set at the street level, permitting direct access to the street from the garage. The basement entrance hall is connected to the first floor by a spiral staircase, while the first floor front entrance is approached from a staircase from the south.

The space devoted to tea-ceremonies is located in the rear of the site, connected to the house by a bridge. The exterior concrete box houses the wooden cross latticework construction of the tea-ceremony room. The walls of the surrounding corridors feature the four paintings of the "Water Fall" series (spring, summer, fall, and winter) by leading Japanese New York-based painter Hiroshi Senjyu.

The paintings can be enjoyed through wooden cross latticework walls of the tearoom. The tearoom is lit naturally by the Japanese traditional ajiro, or basketweave ceiling, in daytime, and at night, like a starry sky, through small holes.

Outside-In House

Marin County, California, USA
Pfau Architecture Ltd

House area: 2,300 square feet/214 square meters
Site area: 2.5 acres/1 hectare
Materials: Concrete, stainless steel, maple, birch, Douglas fir, glass, aluminum, glass mosaic tiles, cedar

The house sits on a stand of ancient Oak trees and looks out over sweeping views of the valley below and far views of the Marin coastal range. The modest original structure was built and inhabited by Rosalind Watkins, a Bay Area architect in the 1950s. Sensing and evoking the splendors of the surroundings, a design was developed for a transparent home that drew the outside spaces inside and responded to the inherent geometry of the existing structure.

All the living space walls were eliminated in the renovation, providing flowing space for daily life. The boomerang shape of the original plan had a strong form that was a result of the intersection of two linear wings. In order for the addition to celebrate these inherent qualities it needed to take place at the heart of the intersection. Each wing of the boomerang was then extended to form overlapping rectangles that went upwards at the intersection, creating a master bedroom addition on the second level.

The new roof forms became simple, layered horizontal extensions of the rest of the existing house. The structural support was left as exposed steel, painted to match the nearby Golden Gate Bridge. Existing steel beams were left "flying" through the dining area to support the new stair and frame a custom-made dining table. To achieve a transparent ladder-like feel, as if climbing in trees, the new stair was made of steel with open risers and stainless steel marine cables.

Poole Residence

Lake Weyba, Queensland, Australia
Gabriel & Elizabeth Poole Design Company

The clients, after having lived in a steel and canvas tent, which was an experience to be remembered for a lifetime, initially set out to design a more practical version but one that retains the quality of light, freedom of spirit, and ventilation controls which made the tent so memorable.

The new house was designed on a lightweight portal system, but walls were now more solid and extensive use was made of the alcove system used on earlier house, this time they were used for wardrobes, kitchen sinks, and bathrooms.

The roof was to be an advancement on the tent, and was selected because of its cooling quality, with an outer fly over an inner roof creating a cushion of cool air which flows between the two surfaces. The house retains the PVC outer fly used in the tent and substitutes a twin wall of polycarbonate sheet for the canvas roof ceiling. The roof ceiling is better insulated as the polycarbonate behaves in much the same way as double glazing while at the same time retain the wonderful luminosity of the ceiling and quality of light throughout the house.

Puente Soivio

Vammala, Finland
Siren Architects Ltd

Client: Leena and Antti Soivio

Up the hillside from the villa is a spring that never runs dry, even in the hottest summer. The couple owning the farm felt that both sides of the stream were desirable locations for the villa, so they decided to build the villa spanning the stream, reflecting the spirit of a bridge.

At the request of the owner, the pond beneath the bridge was stocked with salmon for fishing. The 2-meter-deep pond allows bathers to take a dip straight from the sauna terrace in the middle of the bridge, facing the evening sun. Though the villa is in the middle of a forest, one can sit inside and have the same experience as waking in the morning on a sailing boat, and watching the sun's rays on the ceiling.

Riparian House

St Lucia, Queensland, Australia
The Cox Group

House area: 5,812 square feet/540 square meters
Site area: 8,170 square feet/759 square meters
Materials: Zinc cladding, zinc soffit, vertical western red cedar boarding, horizontal timber battens, stainless steel gutters, Zincalume roofing, stainless steel window mullions, frameless glazing, "off form" colored reinforced concrete walls, sandstone paving

The Riparian House is built around an existing structural frame which cantilevers out over the river bank, affording exceptional views up and down the reach.

It transforms from a lightweight expression over this structure to a masonry expression on flat terrain, zinc cladding and pre-colored concrete, generating a textural resonance between raw materials. Natural timber battening and stacked glass are further treatments used in distinct panels so that an interplay of orthogonal geometries between plan and form is established.

The transition of materials also reflects a sequencing of visually continuous but spatially defined zones from arrival to river edge. While the house is primarily designed for a semi-retired couple, the courtyard "zone" offering its own environment allows for their children to return for visits.

The riverfront portion is vertically layered into upper level master bedroom suite, middle level, and lower level guest accommodation. On the middle level, the cantilever portion is treated as a "living room verandah" via a mechanised glass wall, which lowers to balustrade height, with separate controls for sun and insect protection.

Roof-Roof House

Ampang, Selangor, Malaysia
T.R. Hamzah & Yeang Sdn. Bhd.

Client: Dr K Yeang
House area: 3,500 square feet/325 square meters
Site area: 6,500 square feet/604 square meters
Materials: Brick, precast concrete, louvers, gypsum plaster ceilings, suspended plasterboard ceiling, concrete floor, ceramic tiles

The house is designed as a life-size working prototype of the architect's bioclimatic design ideas. The design is a systemic effort to use climatic factors to shape the building's enclosure, its configuration, and spatial organization.

For instance, its north–south orientation protects the major spaces from the tropical sun. The ground floor living spaces face the east and open to the pool, which takes advantage of the southeast to northwest wind to modify the microclimate. This prevailing wind is cooled as it traverses over the pool water before entering the living spaces, where four movable layers of parts—sliding grilles, glass panels, solid panels, and adjustable blinds—are provided to control the microclimate of the living spaces.

The planning of the internal space follows a radial configuration along an east–west axis, and in this way integrates the spaces between the building and the site boundary wall as mini-courtyards.

Roth Residence

Oakland, California, USA
Ace Architects

Client: David Roth
House area: 3,000 square feet/279 square meters
Materials: Cedar plywood and lumber, colored stucco, copper-faced shingles

An appealing 1920's chalet-style bungalow had stood on the site, but had burned to its foundations in the 1991 Oakland Hills firestorm. The client, whose nearby house had also burned, came to an early meeting with a sketch plan of a courtyard dwelling oriented towards the view—this was a felicitous diagram.

The residence is organized in three blocks set around a courtyard where an open side faces San Francisco Bay. In addition to their domestic purpose, these blocks stand for the recurring pattern of building, inhabiting, and calamity in the Oakland Hills.

The street-fronting block, stucco, and timber with wide overhanging eaves, formally resembles the chalet-style predecessor. The library tower, clad in blackened copper shingles, recalls the charred monolithic chimneys which were the new landmarks after the fire. Across the courtyard, the third block, with its exoskeleton of wood-framing members and plywood, appears to be under construction.

The red stone courtyard, designed to provide for the outdoors, is crisscrossed by the concrete foundations of the earlier house. From the court's heart springs a long narrow runnel extending towards the Bay and reflecting it. Here, sparked by the client, flames can be made to dance across the placid water.

Rotunda House

Nichada Thani Village, Nothaburi, Thailand
Architects 49

Client: Raymond Eaton
House area: 12,917 square feet/1,200 square meters
Materials: Reinforced concrete, painted plastered brick wall with exposed concrete, aluminum composite panel wall cladding

The house occupies a corner location in a housing compound that enforces a policy forbidding homeowners to erect individual fences around their property. As such, creating a private atmosphere, especially around the pool area, has been one of the foremost considerations in designing the house. The resulting design features rooms which have doors and windows which can be closed, such as the living room, the family room, the dining room, and the service areas. The swimming pool is in an enclosed court in order to maximize its privacy.

The master bedroom, the room most heavily utilized by the owner, has been placed in a central position and enjoys a good view of the interior of the house. Elevated above the pool, it creates a shady shelter for swimmers in the pool and at the same time, becomes an arresting focal point.

Geometric forms such as rectangles, squares, and circles were engaged to form the building components; by interlocking, interpenetrating, and creating a dialogue with one another, they served to unify the plan, the façades as well as the sections. The primary material used in the exterior of the house, especially the columns and beams, is exposed concrete, which reflects purity in the use of materials. As for the landscaping, the trees have been planted in key locations.

Roxbury Drive Residence

Beverly Hills, California, USA
Arxis Design Studio

Design team: Leonardo Umansky and Ramiro Diazgranados
House area: 9,000 square feet/836 square meters
Materials: Pace furniture, redwood slats, Douglas fir wood doors and window trim, redwood cabinets and shelves, polishing granite floors, limestone flooring, bamboo plantings, pocket sliding doors

The plan of the house has a modern aesthetic feeling, yet it has a more traditional material palette. Each of the rooms is separated by change of materials on the floor or the creation of a threshold through lower ceiling heights and asymmetrical arches, rather than by conventional means. For instance, the formal living room and family room are divided by a bar that is flanked by two pivoting, 8-foot-wide Douglas fir wood doors. When the panels are closed, each room is clearly defined. However, when the panels are open, the bar serves as an island joining both rooms for large social gatherings. Likewise, floor-to-ceiling glass walls around the breakfast and family rooms slide into pockets, blurring the lines between interior and exterior.

With the house as one massive object, the designers used clever ways to bring natural light into the space. On the northwest corner of the house, the second floor is pushed inward and a perimeter skylight was installed. Light-wells were created to bring light to central parts of the house that would otherwise be dark. The use of clerestories in all rooms brings light into the space, giving the spaces a sense of openness and lightness, while maintaining privacy.

Shapiro Residence

Santa Monica Canyon, California, USA
Ray Kappe, FAIA

House area: 3,900 square feet/362 square meters
Site area: 7,000 square feet/650 square meters
Materials: Steel, concrete, glass

This concrete and steel house evolved through the necessity to provide a series of concrete retaining walls as the house steps up a 40-degree slope. The desire for maximum glass to provide view and deck access was satisfied by the use of the steel rigid frames. The existing garage and first floor of an existing house were maintained, and new concrete walls paralleling the front and side yard setbacks were added to maximize these existing spaces and provide privacy for the entry level court.

The consistent minimum material palette, concrete floors, and monochromatic color scheme provide a minimalist quality to the interiors as they step up the hill to maximum height. This progression up, to, and through the various levels is sequenced with a series of stairs beginning at the entry gate and rising up to the entrance court and glass entry door. The next set of stairs arrives at the major space of the residence, which includes the living room, dining room, and kitchen. Finally one encounters a final stairway that continues past the entrance to the master bedroom, out a rear glass door and up to the pool pavilion.

The house was originally designed for a bachelor who wanted the entry-level rooms to serve as an office and guest bedroom, and include a private court where he could engage in tai chi. The master bedroom, dressing, and bath were placed on the third level. Having married since, the couple now has a small child and the original office area is now the child's room.

Silverman Residence

Los Angeles, California, USA
Rockefeller l Hricak Architects

Client: Tamara and Jay Silverman
House area: 6,900 square feet/641 square meters
Site area: .45 acres/18.2 hectares
Materials: Redwood siding, exterior cement plaster, UV-filtered glass, stainless steel railings and canopies, plaster walls, hardwood, tile, carpet, stone

The site for this residence is located in Rustic Canyon, a unique and historic area that is bordered by the Pacific Ocean and Santa Monica Canyon, the Pacific Palisades, and the Sunset Rivera section of West Los Angeles.

The house is designed on three floors to accommodate the level changes on the property and to allow all important rooms to open directly onto the landscape.

The main living level is raised up above the street allowing for views and privacy. A two-story gallery is the main circulation area and separates the active areas of living, solarium/seating, dining, kitchen, and pantries from the sleeping area with the two bedrooms, each with its private full bath. A small service area includes a powder room, closet, and dumbwaiter.

Located on the first level is a three-car garage and storage area. The remainder is dedicated to family-type entertaining. The bedrooms function as guest quarters or a maid's room. The upper level is reserved for the master bedroom suite. A series of glass doors lead to a spacious balcony facing the ocean.

Skywood House

Middlesex, UK
Graham Phillips, Architect

Client: The Phillips family

The design brief was an evolutionary process. It initially started as an ambition to create a "magical" glass home in a woodland setting where inside/outside would be as dematerialized as possible both by day and night.

This developed to include water as a central theme, to create the joy of a lakeside setting. Other key preferences were to see the house at a distance on arrival, approach by a long drive, and arrive in a courtyard experience. Also, bedrooms to relate to a more private, softer walled garden, and to provide an energy-efficient solution whilst achieving maximum transparency. The husband and wife clients both delight in the "minimalist" aesthetic and the challenge was to achieve this both internally and externally at the same time as providing an entirely practical home for three children and various pets.

The end result is a unique dynamic experience that starts at the entrance gates and unfolds as one moves through a sequence of spaces—of external and internal rooms. Extreme efforts have been made to co-ordinate all details both technically and geometrical not as any end in themselves but to achieve a visual simplicity and expression of form.

Sloan Residence

Bloomfield Hills, Michigan, USA
McIntosh Poris Associates

Client: Richard and Sheila Sloan
House area: 9,000 square feet/836 square meters
Site area: 2.5 acres/1 hectare
Materials: Brick, cedar wood siding, mahogany windows, mahogany doors, limestone, Corten steel, drywall and plaster, slate, bluestone in patios and outdoors, glass mosaic tiles in master bath, cherry wood paneling in sitting room

The project started as a renovation and addition to a 1953 house. After a series of alternative schemes for renovation and addition were considered, it was decided to tear the house down and build a new house on the site. The two-story house features a large open living/dining room, morning room, breakfast area, master suite with separate sitting room, three guest bedrooms, third-floor office/study with 360-degree views, screening room, exercise room, and two covered porches overlooking Long Lake.

The architects designed a house that is about its relationship to the landscape: the house comes out of the hill it is set into. It is set back from the road, and is approached on a drive supported by Corten-steel retaining walls coming out of the earth. The walls frame views of the house and landscape upon approach from the drive court and entry. From the entry, one can see through the living room, out the back to Long Lake. Every room has a view to the lakes and the landscape.

The design was intentionally kept subdued and subtle, always emphasizing the strength of the landscape outside. Interior elements, such as columns, walls, baseboards, doors, and windows are delineated in mahogany wood. Furniture is primarily modern, including Bauhaus classics, 1970's acrylic mod, Maya Lin chairs, an original Hans Wegner chair, a chair by Wegner's teacher upholstered in 140-year-old fabric, and streamlined contemporary mixed with eclectic antiques, as well as a few pieces and built-ins designed by McIntosh Poris.

Terner Residence and Entenza Remodel

Pacific Palisades, California, USA
Barry A. Berkus, AIA

House area: Terner House (new) 6,523 square feet/606 square meters; Entenza House (renovation) 2,315 square feet/215 square meters
Site area: 1.02 acres/0.4 hectares

In the late 1940s John Entenza, publisher of *Arts and Architecture* magazine, commissioned Charles Eames and Eero Saarinen to design his own home as part of A&A Case Study Program. The resulting Case Study House #9 was sited across a blufftop meadow opposite Eames' own home, overlooking the Pacific Ocean. Within this historic context, the clients acquired the Entenza property, desiring to build a residence for themselves while re-establishing the integrity of the deteriorated Entenza Home. Careful planning revitalized the Entenza structure as an independent guesthouse connected to the new dwelling by a series of architectural blades.

The Entenza House was in disrepair with multiple additions added over the years, covering the core and camouflaging its original design statement. Considerable research enabled the structure to be restored. Although many of the original materials were out of production, systems were painstakingly re-manufactured to replace deteriorated components important to the original statement.

The new residence pays homage to modernity through the incorporation of cubist forms expressing the volumetrics as structural components of the home. Each cube form is coded by color and carefully conceived not to subordinate the Entenza structure, but to create an architectural courtyard allowing each structure to enhance the other.

The Ledge House

Catoctin Mountains, Maryland, USA
Bohlin Cywinski Jackson

House area: 4,252 square feet/395 square meters
Site area: 198 acres/80 hectares
Materials: Quartzite stone, galvanised steel, white cedar, western red cedar, Douglas fir, mahogany

Placed at the edge of a small plateau on a forested mountainside, the house overlooks a stream valley to the south. By employing the logs, heavy timbers and stonework found in rustic buildings of the early 1900s and arranging the new structure along the south rim of the cut, a remarkably evocative forespace is created.

The natural look of the log timber construction on the exterior of the house gives the illusion of the structure growing out from the forest. Hand-peeled, scribed-in-place, white cedar logs were chosen for their naturally rot and insect-resistant characteristics. In contrast, the interior of the structure employs select, structural grade, Douglas fir dimensional timbers, rafters, columns and beams selected for visual and structural qualities.

Using heavy timber post and beam construction enables the exterior walls to be free of load bearing and therefore very flexible in design. Large glazed mahogany-framed window walls along with western red cedar siding add to the visual richness of the exterior.

Tree House

Balmoral, Sydney, Australia
Lippman Associates

This site is located in a thickly wooded reserve in close proximity to Middle Harbour in the northern suburbs of Sydney. The site slopes steeply from a gravel track down to the north where it adjoins a park. Access from the gravel track allowed all the living areas and bedrooms to fan out to the sun and views. The house relates to the terrain, stepping down and across the site over five levels.

On the top floor the master bedroom and office float in the tree tops, high above the ground, enjoying privacy and unimpeded views through dense vegetation and to the harbor. The entry level accommodates kitchen, dining, and sunroom with a living area on a sunken/split level. A two-car garage is also provided at this level. Two split lower levels accommodate the children's bedrooms and play areas. The different floor levels are connected by an open tread staircase wrapped in translucent glass, which acts as a pivot.

In order to minimize the intrusion on the site, a steel framing system was developed which allowed the house to hover above the terrain. The house was loosely organized around a 6 by 6 meter structural grid which established a series of pods to accommodate and express the various spaces and activities in the house. The structure is feathered at the edges by way of cantilevers to reinforce a sense of weightlessness.

Trillium Springs Farmhouse

New Buffalo, Michigan, USA
Nagle Hartray Danker Kagan McKay Architects Planners

House area: 4,000 square feet/372 square meters

The site is several hundred acres of fields that are farmed by the owner. An artificial pond provides the foreground to the south-facing home with heavy woods surrounding the fields.

The building complex is composed of the two-story, three-bedroom main house; a guesthouse with sleeping loft connected with a screen porch; and the garage and farm office connected with a porte cochere/trellis. The L-shaped house is protected by sunscreens on the view side with decks and roof terraces which extend the space outdoors. Diagonal views through the first floor expand the visual space. The stone kitchen fire stove and wooden stair anchor the composition.

A screen porch with screen roof provides an outdoor room between guest quarters and entry. All exterior walls and trellises are natural-finish clear cedar siding and trim. Chimney, gutters, and downspouts are lead-coated copper. Black metal is used for window frames, railings, and struts. Interior finishes are laminated pine beams and decking, pine window trim and doors, maple cabinets and furnishings, and mahogany floors.

Turtle Creek House

Dallas, Texas, USA
Antoine Predock Architect

House area: 11,800 square feet/1,096 square meters

This house, built for enthusiastic bird watchers, is along a prehistoric trail that follows the Austin limestone formation in a landscape where woodlands, prairie, and stream overlap. Anchored limestone ledges were designed in the foreground to allude to geologic presence and ancient memories. These ledges also contain local plant life, encouraging birds to occupy this area.

Located where eastern and western bird habitats converge and along major north-south migratory flyways, the site becomes the vantage point for observation and for participation in an ever-changing pageant. As the house reaches out from its earthbound datum line, it opens into and explores the various levels of avian habitation, the water's edge, the under story, the canopy, and the sky. The central fissure, formalized as an entrance foyer, is the point of departure for access to the various observation vantage points and to the north and south wings.

The south wing is a realm for social gatherings and a private retreat. The north wing is the domain where everyday life unfolds and informal gatherings occur. A third zone of the house, the roofscape, engages the sky. From here walkways over the house, along the top of a rocky outcrop, survey bird habitats, arriving guests, and the Dallas skyline. Moving closer to the parapet, an intimate rooftop arena is revealed which is inwardly focused while also providing a shielded cover for outward viewing. The central steel "sky ramp" projects the entrance fissure into the canopy of trees and beyond to the sky.

Tyler Residence

Tubac, Arizona, USA
Rick Joy Architects

Client: Warren and Rose Tyler
Materials: Concrete, wood, steel, plaster, translucent glass, maple

The site was chosen for its southern orientation towards panoramic views, isolated mountain ranges, and expansive desert landscape. The building site is sloped approximately 10 percent to the south and is covered with scrub, native mesquite trees, and low wild grasses.

A one-bedroom house, with garage, shop and two-bedroom guesthouse was requested by the client. A large linear courtyard is defined by two simple shed forms, which are arranged with orientation towards prime views. The courtyard provides relief from the overwhelmingly expansive setting while the two buildings frame a cropped view of Tumacacori peak—the client's favorite.

The visitor arrives from above the house via gravel road, and is greeted by only the glazed ends of the above-grade portions of the master bedroom, shop, and office, which at night will appear as abstract glowing forms hovering just above the ground.

Guests then descend into the courtyard by way of a stair wedged between the two retaining walls. This courtyard plays an important role in the entry experience with its large shade trees and water features. Planting arrangements and detailing in the courtyard will assert a very refined artificial character. Protruding steel box forms penetrate the building in carefully selected but apparently random locations to frame specific views. A negative edge pool located at the west end of the courtyard expends the experience to the view beyond.

Urban Residence

Laguna Beach, California, USA
Shubin + Donaldson Architects

House area: 4,000 square feet/372 square meters
Site area: 5,970 square feet/555 square meters
Materials: Kal-Wall skylight, metal roofing, Hardiboard siding, plaster, slate tile, maple hardwood flooring, glass, granite countertops, mosaic glass tiles, ashwood cabinetry, Douglas fir ply

This new home emerged from the ashes of the Laguna Beach fire of 1993. Using the opportunity to rebuild, the clients asked for something dramatic to be built on a tight hillside lot overlooking Emerald Bay and the Pacific Ocean. Taking advantage of the 270-degree views of the ocean and coast, the architectural team created a home that meets the contrasting need for formal luxury with laid-back beach living.

Built in a small, steep, downslope, the design was driven by the opportunities and limitations of the site. The house, which is set on an angle to maximize the tight lot, is organized around a wall that stands in the middle of the house. This wall splits the house into communal and private living areas and allows for a vaulted ceiling that organizes the whole upper public area into one large space under a copper roof.

The challenge for the architects was to design the main living areas, kitchen, and master bedroom on the entry level, with three bedrooms below. The owners were concerned that the lower level not feel like it was underground. Through large and small windows, the architects achieved cinematic views of Emerald Bay for all the rooms in the house, and then designed the circulation to flow along the back retaining wall, thus all but eliminating the underground feeling.

Vacation House in Spetses

Island of Spetses, Greece
Meletitiki-Alexandros N. Tombazis and Associates

House area: 2,260 square feet/210 square meters
Site area: 44,671 square feet/4,150 square meters
Materials: Reinforced concrete, brick, wood, ceramic tiles, marble, cobblestone, metal

Spetses is a small, pine-covered island at the entrance of the Gulf of Argolis, 15 miles (24 kilometers) from the coast of the Peleponnese. The house lies on the southeast coastline, and is surrounded by 4,150 square meters (44,671 square feet) of land, which slopes gently southwards to the sea.

The entrance to this property is from the northwest, via a cobblestone path that leads to the wooden gate of the inner courtyard, through which one both enters the house and ascends to the terrace. Passing through the semi-covered spaces of the courtyard and the arcade, the view to the southern courtyard, pool, and the sea is gradually revealed.

The house consists of three rectangular blocks. The two main ones, one with two floors and a tiled room, and the other with one floor, are laid out at right angles defining the main, southeastern, open terrace with the pool. The two buildings are connected at ground level by a semi-covered passage/arcade, on the roof of which a terrace with unimpeded views in all directions is created. The third block is a small pavilion used for dining "al fresco."

Villa le Goff

Marseille, France
Rudy Ricciotti Architecte

House area: 2,368 square feet/220 square meters
Site area: 8,288 square feet/770 square meters

The design goal was to integrate a personal contemporary art collection with the concept of a villa. The residence has been built on the side of a hill where zoning regulations allow a construction height offering views above the tree canopy to the Mediterranean Sea.

Rooms situated over the livable part of the villa take advantage of the teak terrace, which features an in-ground swimming pool. The gallery offers exhibition space with fluorescent lighting integrated into the concrete and polished quartz floor.

An outside curtain, made from camouflage netting, filters light and protects the main façades from the sun.

Villa te Goes

Goes, Netherlands
Bedaux de Brouwer Architecten

House area: 6,964 square feet/647 square meters
Site area: 43,056 square feet/4,000 square meters

The villa is located on the banks of Goese Lake, an artificial lake in the polder between the town of Goes and village of Wilhelminadorp, Netherlands.

The programme of requirements stipulated relatively many functions at ground level: living room, kitchen, entrance, and garages, as well as two bedrooms with en-suite facilities. The programme for the upper floors was comparatively modest: two bedrooms, bathroom, and a small billiards room with fireplace.

The villa borders the most northerly edge of the plot. On the one hand this allows a direct view across the open fields; on the other it maximises the size of the south garden and the distance to the "farmhouse-style" houses.

The building programme is contained in two separate volumes, each with its own height, own architecture, and own materials.

Wakeham House

Rogate, West Sussex, UK
Robert Adam Architects

Client: Harold Carter
House area: 2,745 square feet/255 square meters
Site area: 1.2 acres/0.5 hectares
Materials: Render and stone exterior, timber frame with high thermal insulation, natural slate roof, slate floor

This house was built in memory of the Hon. Brenda Carter, a pioneer of solar energy research. It is built on the site of her previous home, which burnt down in 1968. Brenda Carter worked with Ray Maw, a solar energy specialist, and then with Robert Adam to prepare a new design, which combined classical architecture with the latest developments in the use of passive solar energy. Work continued on the project after her death in 1993 with her son Harold Carter.

In the center of the house a double-height space is heated by direct sunlight, and a natural ventilation system draws warm air and distributes it throughout the building. Sixty percent of the wall surface of the south elevation is triple-glazed, with little glass on the shaded north side. A portico creates deep recesses that shade the rooms in the summer, but which allow warming from the low winter sun. The walls have a timber frame with high thermal insulation, and are clad with rendered brick with natural sandstone detail. The roof is finished in natural slate.

Weissberg Residence

Beverly Hills, California, USA
Belzberg Architects

Client: Max and Diane Weissberg
House area: 3,391 square feet/315 square meters
Materials: Steel frame, wood, steel, troweled plaster, metal roof, glass

This single-family residence is split into two components. One incorporates the mechanical, storage, food preparation, dining, office, and guestroom. The other is dedicated to the clients sleeping and bathing quarters. The collision of the two creates a third zone; this interstitial space is used as the formal living area with the hearth traditionally set at its core. Sectional partitions become an integral device separating and adjoining crucial formal spaces for descriptive events.

In an area steeped in traditional styles this single-family residence introduces a modern vocabulary that both questions and learns from the diverse context surrounding it.

West 22nd Street Residence

Chelsea, New York, USA
Charles Rose Architects

House area: 6,500 square feet/604 square meters
Site area: 5,000 square feet/464 square meters
Materials: Stucco, painted steel, wood windows, lead-coated copper, mahogany decking, plaster walls, maple woodwork, larch floors, Douglas fir ceilings, painted steel

This recently completed project, located in Chelsea, the heart of New York City's new gallery district, creates a gallery space and residence around a unique urban garden. The project includes a retail showroom on the street level, a small rental apartment on the second floor, and a three-level residential space occupying the top floors.

The residence, which wraps around a central garden, is sculptural in form and yet "transparent" enough to incorporate natural light and elements of the landscape into its unified design. Lawns, peastone paths, flower beds, planters, and trellises provide natural sanctuary within an urban setting. The interior space is arranged around open areas that afford ample garden views.

As the residence unfolds spatially, views across the garden from various vantage points create richly layered spaces that intertwine inside and outside, urban and natural, sculptural and organic.

Yudell-Beebe House

Sea Ranch, California, USA
Moore Ruble Yudell

House area: 2,100 square feet/195 square meters
Materials: Concrete, wood, metal, plaster

This house was developed in close response to the rhythms, textures, and materials of the rugged coastal environment of Northern California. Designed by and for an architect and artist couple, they sought to create a place that is refined yet informal, serene and rich with discovery.

Each part of the house responds to its specific site conditions. The east elevation presents a rugged entry, a contemporary interpretation of the western front. The south opens to the ocean with full or partial shading. The west provides screening from houses across the meadow while framing water and rocks through habitable bays. The north is shaped as an intimate court with mountain views. A garden of native grass and rocks suggests a mountain to ocean connection with its implied passage through the center of the house.

Windows are composed to frame near and distant views of the landscape and to celebrate the movement and wash of light. The towers of the studios and chimneys collect light and allow for natural convection, while conforming to the height restriction of the architectural guidelines.

In harmony with its environment, the house celebrates craft and place as a retreat for quiet contemplation or spirited social interaction.

Index

Acknowledgments

IMAGES is pleased to present *100 of the World's Best Houses* to its compendium of design and architectural publications.

We wish to thank Cathy Slessor for kindly sharing her knowledge and expertise in the writing of the introduction for this book.

We would also like to thank all participating firms for their valuable contribution to this publication.